PIANO PLAYGROUND:
Games, Movement, and Group Activities
for
Piano Instruction

Charise A. Lindsay, Ph.D.

Published by

Say Press

P.O. Box 691063

Orlando, FL 32869-1063

Piano Playground: Games, Movement, and Group Activities for Piano Instruction

Copyright © 2014 by Charise A. Lindsay
Printed in the United States of America
All rights reserved. No part of this book shall be reproduced or transmitted in any form or by any means, electronic or mechanical, including photocopying, recording, or by any information or retrieval system, without written permission from:

    Charise A. Lindsay
    P.O. Box 691063
    Orlando, FL 32869

ISBN 978-0-9841491-9-3

Piano Playground: Games, Movement, and Group Activities for Piano Instruction

TO Stan and Linda Lindsay

My Mother—who inspired me as my first piano teacher and
My Father—who inspired me as a Ph.D. and professor

Piano Playground: Games, Movement, and Group Activities for Piano Instruction

Piano Playground: Games, Movement, and Group Activities for Piano Instruction

Table of Contents

Defining Teaching Effectiveness in the Music Classroom 1

Introduction for Teachers 3

Master Checklist 6

Games 7

    Activity 1: Mother May I? 8

    Activity 2: Horse 12

    Activity 3: Prince of Paris 15

    Activity 4: Piano Arcade 19

    Activity 5: Hurdles 23

    Activity 6: Musical Pursuit 26

    Activity 7: Volleyball 29

    Activity 8: Stress Ball Pass 33

    Activity 9: Four Corners 37

    Activity 10: Blues Scale Hopscotch 41

    Activity 11: Scale Fingerings Dominoes 46

    Activity 12: Piano Telephone 50

    Activity 13: Cross Training 54

    Activity 14: I Write the Songs 59

    Activity 15: The Gambler 63

    Activity 16: Charade (Sort Of) 67

    Activity 17: Chord Progression Scrabble 71

    Activity 18: Key Signature War 75

    Activity 19: Pentachord/Scale Game 78

    Activity 20: The Natural (A Baseball Game) 85

    Activity 21: Triad Bingo 89

Movement Activities 93

    Activity 22: Alberti Calisthenics 94

    Activity 23: Shortest Distance Line 98

    Activity 24: Grapevine Run 101

    Activity 25: Ear-Nose Name Game 105

   Activity 26: Brain/Arm Teaser 109

Group Work 113
   Activity 27: The Apprentice 114
   Activity 28: Animated Feature...117
   Activity 29: Make a Scene 120
   Activity 30: Electric Statues 124
   Activity 31: Baroque Imitation 127
   Activity 32: Recreate This Photo 131
   Activity 33: Classical Voices...135
   Activity 34: The Brown Suit..139
   Activity 35: Build a House 143
   Activity 36: Guests at a Party 150

References..152
Concept Index 154

Introduction

Defining Teaching Effectiveness in the Music Classroom

It is important for music educators to be aware of the important factors that contribute to teaching effectiveness in the music classroom. Music education researchers have emphasized nonverbal communication and enthusiasm, active learning, and complete teaching patterns. When these three factors are reduced to their most important elements, a macrocosm/microcosm relationship emerges. It is important for teachers to present their information accurately and with enthusiasm. This is Teacher Delivery or Teacher Presentation. In addition, many studies suggest that the more that the students are actively participating in a class, the better are the attitudes, attentiveness, and even achievement. So the second factor can be called Activity. The final factor comes from the idea of a complete teaching pattern. Step One of a complete teaching pattern, which is teacher presentation, has already been addressed as the first factor contributing to teaching effectiveness. The second step is the student response. This is the activity portion of a complete teaching pattern, and the second factor for effective teaching. The final step is feedback. This has not been addressed in the other two factors. So, the third factor is feedback from the teacher. The macrocosm contains the three effectiveness factors: teacher delivery, activity, and teacher feedback. The microcosm is represented by a three-step complete teaching pattern.

Much of the research supports the importance of the use of activity. Student activity seems to improve attentiveness, attitudes, and achievement. In addition, there have been several studies that support the use of complete teaching patterns. Activity is an essential step in a complete teaching pattern. Without it, the teaching pattern is incomplete. Furthermore, results of some studies may suggest that activity is the main element in a complete teaching pattern. Piano students in Siebenaler's (1997) study received higher performance scores from judges when their teachers moved quickly through several complete teaching patterns. This allowed students several opportunities for activity or performance. These students were involved in performance or activity for more total time during their lessons than the students who received lower scores from the judges. This suggests that more student activity assists in musical/academic achievement.

The factor contributing to teaching effectiveness called Teacher Delivery includes nonverbal communication skills and affect. Incorporating activities into the classroom may naturally produce more teacher affect. Games and other creative activities may not feel as formal to the teacher or student. Therefore, a teacher may relax into the delivery, allowing natural facial expressions, gestures, and vocal modulation to emerge. These nonverbal communication skills have been cited as variables contributing to effective teaching (Hamann, et al., 2000; Hendel, 1995; Madsen, 1990, Sims, 1986).

Teacher Delivery promotes higher attentiveness among students (Sims, 1986; and Yarbrough & Price, 1981). It can be argued that nonverbal communication skills and affect are tools used to increase students' interest in the subject. In other words, these skills engage students. Creative activities and games to teach musical concepts may also make students more interested. Therefore, nonverbal communication and affect, while still important, may be bolstered by activities. Essentially, Activity and Teacher Delivery seemingly can work together to create a more effective learning situation. In light of these observations, this book has been written to help teachers engage students in group or private piano by providing creative activities that present musical and pianistic concepts.

Introduction for Teachers

The following introduction is intended for use in conjunction with the resource activity sheets. This introduction and the Master Checklist for Teachers should be read prior to using the activity sheets in order to understand the idea behind the activity sheets. To be an effective piano teacher, one must utilize techniques that teachers use in other musical settings, like choirs, orchestras, and other private lessons. According to research, there are three major elements that make an effective teacher (Blocher, Greenwood, & Shellahamer, 1997; Dunn, 1997; and Madsen, 1990). The first element is "teacher presentation." This includes the information being presented, and the manner in which it is presented. The second element is "student activity." Many studies have shown that, when students are actively engaged in a lesson, they are more attentive, have better attitudes, and achieve more. The third and final element includes complete teaching patterns, and ultimately feedback.

Complete teaching patterns contain three steps which are like the three major elements, but on a smaller scale. Step One is "teacher delivery." To be most effective in this step, it is important to give accurate musical or academic information, rather than simply giving a direction (such as "play that section again," or "try page five."). The second step is the "student response." If you ask a question, then the students will answer during the "student response" step. If you explain that a certain piece of music should be played *forte*, then the students will play the piece during this step. Step Three is "teacher feedback." During this step, you will let the students know if their answers to the questions are right or wrong, or you will state whether or not their performances were *forte*. Research done on complete teaching patterns often shows that specific feedback is more effective than nonspecific feedback (Bowers, 1997; Goolsby, 1997; Hendel, 1995; Sibenaler, 1997; and Speer, 1994). Also, approvals (or positive feedback) are usually preferred over disapprovals (negative feedback) (Duke, 1999/2000; Madsen & Duke, 1993; and Price, 1992). There is still some debate whether approvals are always more effective than disapprovals, but specific approvals and specific disapprovals are almost always more effective than nonspecific approvals and disapprovals. In other words, it is better to explain why something was performed incorrectly than to just say, "not quite," about a performance that was played incorrectly.

The first major element, "teacher presentation" involves using nonverbal communication skills. These skills include eye contact, facial expressions, physical appearance, (vocalics) vocal quality, (kinesics) body movements, (proxemics) location, and physical contact. You must make eye contact with those you are teaching to help keep them engaged in your instruction. Your facial expressions should vary throughout the lesson, showing enthusiasm and other appropriate emotions. If your physical appearance represents someone who is well-groomed and fairly fashionable, your teaching may be more effective (Berko, Rosenfeld, & Samover, 1997; and Lindsay, 2004). Along with facial expressions, your vocal inflection should also vary according to your emotions. The pitch should be on the higher, middle portion of your voice's natural range. Try not to speak too quickly, or too slowly.

The next three skills involved the space that your body uses. Your body movements can help keep students' attention. Use movements that have specific meanings (emblems), such as nodding your head, clapping your hands, and shrugging your shoulders. Even movements that do not contain specific meanings, but clarify a concept (illustrators) can be useful. Examples of these movements are pointing at an object or specific direction, modeling a piano skill, demonstrating a dance step, and using hand and arm gestures to indicate the size of something.

Varying your location in the room can be effective as well. Move to different parts of the room, standing a little closer to different students at different times. It may be necessary to move into a student's personal space in order to move an arm or hand into an appropriate piano-playing position. Also, be sure the room is arranged to be conducive to learning.

Essentially, remember that you are a performer. You are writer, director, producer, and actor. You write the lesson plans, guide students through the lesson, prepare the materials and classroom, and must demonstrate appropriate behaviors and attitudes. Sometimes the director must tell the actors exactly what facial expressions and movements to make. S/he may need to demonstrate as well. Your class is like a movie production. Sometimes, it is a one-person show with audience participation. Sometimes it is a "cast of thousands." All activities in this book are written with a movie theme. Each activity sheet contains a "Spotlight," "Props & Set Design," " Story Board," "Encore," "Important Plot Points," "Behind the Scenes," and "The Script." There is also a reminder, "Don't Forget! Lights, camera [This is presentation] Action [This is the activity and student response] Applause" [This is (approval) feedback]. Some of the activities also have a "Re-makes" and "Credits" section.

The "Spotlight" lists the piano skills and music concepts that the activity addresses. "Props & Set Design" lists the materials necessary to perform this activity, and how to build the materials, if necessary. The "Story Board," explains how to perform the activity. The "Encore" section lists piano exercises to perform as a follow-up. Explanations of how to keep students active, provide student feedback, and some nonverbal communication skills are listed in the "Important Plot Points." "Behind the Scenes" provides suggestions on how to keep things "action-packed" (pacing), clothing recommendations, a reminder to vary your facial expressions, and rehearsal suggestions to help ensure that approvals (positive feedback) occur more often than disapprovals (negative feedback).

"The Script" emphasizes complete teaching patterns. There is a scripted sample of a possible complete teaching pattern that could occur while performing this activity. If there are possible alterations that could be made to the activity, these are listed under the "Re-makes" section. The "Credits" section is included if the idea for the activity came from another source.

Master Checklist

1. Are you presenting the musical and academic information accurately?

2. Are you making eye contact with the students?

3. Are you using varied facial expressions?

4. How is your physical appearance? Do you have good posture? Have you followed proper personal hygiene procedures? Is your clothing professional and generally in style?

5. How is your vocal quality? Are you speaking at an audible, clear volume? Are you speaking too quickly or too slowly? Do you vary your vocal inflection (voice pitch)?

6. How are your kinesics? Are you using emblems such as nodding your head, applauding, and shrugging your shoulders? Are you using illustrators like pointing, demonstrating, sizing, modeling, and cupping the ear?

7. How are your proxemics? Is the room set-up conducive to learning? Are the students to follow a seating arrangement? Are the temperature, lighting, and view pleasant? Are you utilizing public space, social space, and some personal space (but not intimate space) of the students?

8. Are you using only appropriate physical contact?

9. Is the pacing of the lesson quick enough to keep students' attention?

10. Are you allowing the students to perform or be actively involved most of the time?

11. Are you using complete teaching patterns?

    1. Teacher Delivery (Musical/academic information preferred over giving directions)

    2. Student Response (Answer a question or follow a direction)

    3. Teacher Feedback (Approval is often preferred over disapproval. Specific

feedback is always preferred over nonspecific feedback (like "good," "not quite," etc.).

Games

Game One

Activity 1: Mother, May I?

Spotlight: Transposing simple melodies and musical examples

Props & Set Design:

- ✓ Simple melodies and musical examples to be transposed.

Story Board:

1. The goal of this activity is to practice transposing musical examples by baby steps (half steps), steps (major seconds), and giant steps (minor thirds). Students will gradually continue up the keyboard (from their last key) until they have transposed the melody one octave.
2. The game is played like the traditional "Mother, May I" children's game. Everyone starts in the example's written key. The teacher is Mother. Mother calls out to the first person, "Take [insert number] [insert type] steps forward."
3. For example:
   "Take 3 baby steps forward."
4. With this example, the first person must ask "Mother, May I." Then the teacher answers, "Yes you may." The student then transposes the melody up a half step, three times. This means that the student plays the melody three times during this turn.

5. The first student must then wait until the rest of the students take their first turn. When his/her turn comes again, s/he starts from the ending key.
6. For example:
   If the original key is C major, three baby (half) steps up is D#/E-flat. This is the starting key for student's next turn.
7. At each successive turn, pick up at the previous key. Once the student has transposed all the way up to one octave higher than the original key, s/he is finished.
8. If the student forgets to say "Mother, may I," s/he must go all the way back to the original key.

Re-makes:

Alter the distance that the students must travel before completing the activity (Two octaves instead of one.) and/or alter the size of baby steps, steps, and giant steps.

If students are concerned about fairness, the teacher can draw the number and size of steps from a hat. This makes it more random. One hat may contain the numbers. The other may hold the sizes of the steps.

Don't Forget!!!

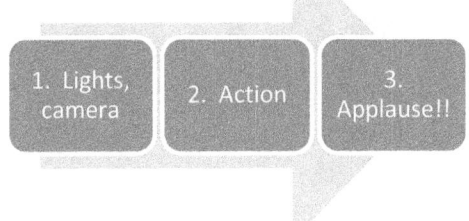

1. Lights, camera
2. Action
3. Applause!!

Games

Important Plot Points

1. <u>Student Action</u> - Playing the musical examples in new keys.

2. <u>Specific Feedback</u> - Double check accidentals for new keys.

3. <u>Stunt Work</u> - Demonstrate and explain how to progress "three baby steps."

Behind the Scenes

1. **Action-packed.** Keep the musical examples short.

2. **Costuming**

3. **Facial Expressions** Think Silent Films.

4. **Sound System** - State clearly the command for each student..

5. **Rehearsal** - Allow students to practice the example in its original key so that they are confident.

Also, the first round should only be one or two measures long, or stay within a five-finger pattern.

Page 10

The Script:

> *The teacher will conduct several complete teaching patterns resembling the following script. They will follow this format:*
>
> 1. Ask students to take two steps forward.
>
> 2. Give time for student response.
>
> 3. Teacher Feedback = Make sure the correct key signatures are implemented in the new, transposed keys.
>
>
> Teacher: "Take one giant step forward."
>
> Student Response = SR
>
> Teacher Feedback: "One giant step is a minor third. That means that your new key should be E-flat major."

Game Two

Activity 2: Horse

Spotlight: Reviewing pieces, skills, and musical excerpts that have been covered during the course.

Props & Set Design:

- ✓ The exercises and musical pieces on which the classes have been working.
- ✓ Metronome

Story Board:

1. The goal of this game is to be the last person to accumulate the letters, H, O, R, S, and E to spell the word, "horse." The game is played like the basketball game of the same name.
2. Divide the class into small groups. Each group plays their own game of "Horse." Decide the order in which each student will play. The first person gets to choose the first "shot."
3. The "shots" must only be a few measures long. The first person "shoots" (plays a musical exercise, or portion of a musical piece.). If the shot is successful, then the next player must play the same excerpt in the same tempo and with the correct hand(s). If the shot is a scale or arpeggio, the same fingering must also be used. If the second player is successful, the next player must play the same excerpt. This continues until someone makes a mistake or it is the first player's turn again (whichever comes first.).

4. If someone makes a mistake, that player gets a letter (starting with H). The next player in line then gets to choose the next shot. If no one makes a mistake and it is the first player's turn again, the first player gets to choose a new shot.
5. When a player gets all of the letters in the word, "horse," s/he is out. The last person to spell "horse" wins.

Re-makes:

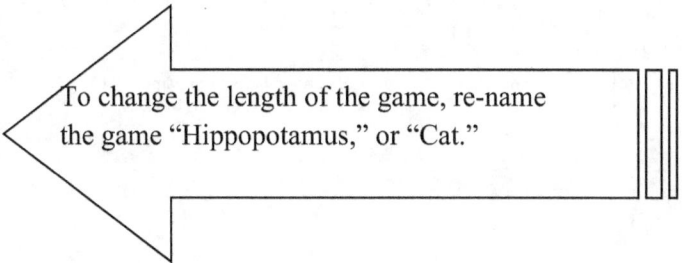

To change the length of the game, re-name the game "Hippopotamus," or "Cat."

Don't Forget!!!

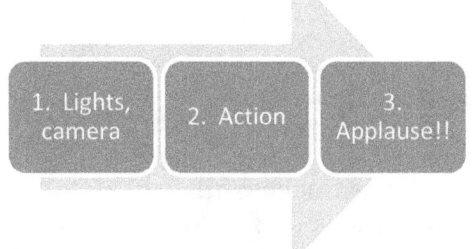

1. Lights, camera
2. Action
3. Applause!!

Important Plot Points

| 1. <u>Student Action</u> - Taking the "shots" to keep from getting a letter. | 2. <u>Specific Feedback</u> - Make sure students are using the correct fingerings and tempos. | 3. <u>Stunt Work</u> - Demonstrate a few "shots" before the groups begin their games. |

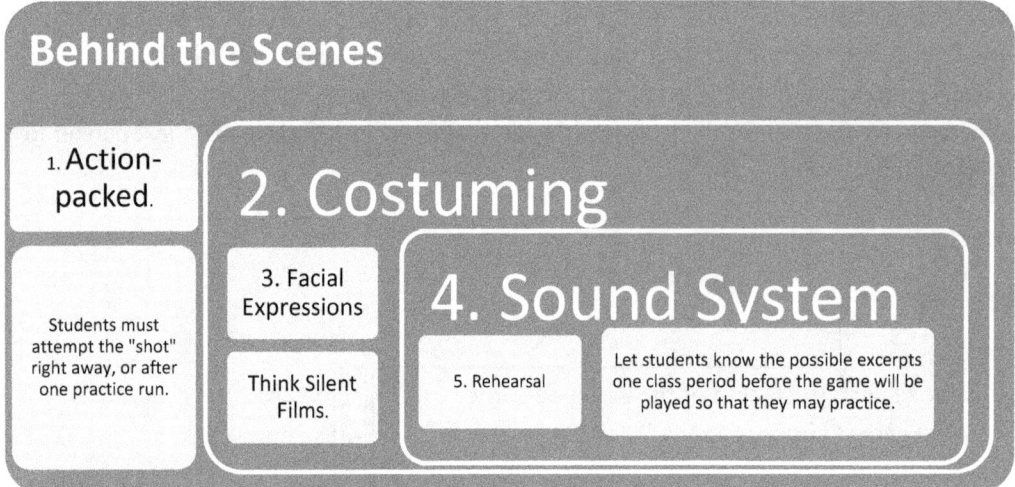

The Script:

> *The teacher will conduct several complete teaching patterns resembling the following script. S/he will follow this format:*
>
> 1. Ask students to select a shot, tempo, and hand.
>
> 2. Give time for student response.
>
> 3. Teacher Feedback = Correct wrong fingerings, notes, and tempos.
>
> Teacher: "Jessica played the first excerpt and was successful. Now Craig, who is second, must play the same thing with both hands, and at a quarter note = 120.
>
> Student Response = SR
>
> Teacher Feedback: "Since the left hand dropped out in the second measure, you now get an "H."

Game Three

Activity 3: Prince of Paris

Spotlight: Sight-reading

Props & Set Design:

- ✓ Sight-reading exercises that are *easy* to *medium* difficulty. The exercises should either be one page in length or be repeated.

Story Board:

1. The goal of this activity is to get students to start playing quickly, and then to continue, regardless of errors made while playing. Students will have to pay close attention to the progress of the game, as well as the place in the music.
2. Each student is assigned a number, except one student. The last student (in the back of the room) is placed at "the foot." While a student is at "the foot," s/he does not have an opportunity to play part of the sight-reading exercise. However, "the foot" must still pay attention to the music in case s/he has an opportunity to move out of the foot.
3. The teacher leads the activity. S/he starts by saying, "Prince of Paris lost his hat and blamed it on number two [or insert another number here]. Number two [insert another number here] to the foot."

4. While the teacher is saying, "Number two to the foot," the student who is assigned to number two must begin playing the first measure of the sight-reading exercise. The student must not wait until after that statement is finished, otherwise s/he must go to the foot. If s/he starts playing the music in time, the teacher answers by playing measure 2. The student then responds with measure 3. The teacher plays measure 4, then the student calls out a number of another student (For example, number eleven.). The teacher says, "Number eleven to the foot." Number eleven must start playing measure 5 before this statement is completed. If not, s/he must move to the foot. If number eleven is successful, the teacher answers by playing measure 6. The student plays measure 7, then the teacher plays measure 8. Next the student calls out a new number of another student. With each new student, the sight-reading exercise progresses forward four measures.
5. If a student gets sent to the foot (for example, number eleven), all students behind that student move up one place. Student twelve is now student eleven. Student thirteen is now student twelve, and so on. Student eleven is now the foot.
6. The teacher restarts the game by saying, "Prince of Paris lost his hat and blamed it on number two [or insert another number here]. Number two [insert another number here] to the foot." Student two must begin playing where the activity left off before student eleven was sent to the foot.
7. The activity continues until the teacher decides to end it.
8. This is a strong exercise in concentration and looking ahead in sight-reading.

Encore!!

Allow students to sight-read pieces at their ability levels..

Don't Forget!!!

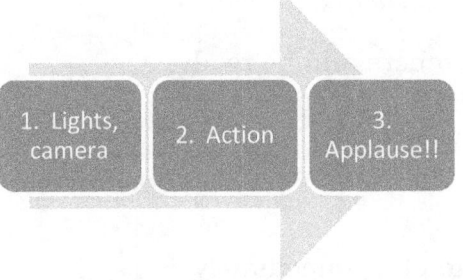

1. Lights, camera
2. Action
3. Applause!!

Important Plot Points

1. <u>Student Action</u> - Playing portions of the sight-reading exercise, and moving to new keyboards.

2. <u>Specific Feedback</u> - Encouraging students to keep playing even if they make mistakes.

3. <u>Stunt Work</u> - Demonstrate playing portions of the music before the statement is complete.

Behind the Scenes

1. **Action-packed.**

Due to the nature of this activity, students will have to pay close attention to keep up.

2. Costuming

3. Facial Expressions

Think Silent Films.

4. Sound System - Speak loudly and clearly when calling out which number is to go to the foot.

5. Rehearsal

Begin with an easy exercise so that students get used to the rest of the activity.

The Script:

> *The teacher will conduct several complete teaching patterns resembling the following script. They will follow this format:*
>
> 1. Ask students to keep track of their numbers and be ready to play, should their number be called. Begin the game and call out a number.
>
> 2. Give time for student response.
>
> 3. Teacher Feedback = Remind student to play immediately and keep going even if s/he makes a mistake.
>
> Teacher: "Number five to the foot."
>
> Student Response = SR
>
> Teacher Feedback: (Since the student began playing before you finished your statement and kept playing, play the next measure in the music.)

Game Four

Activity 4: Piano Arcade

Spotlight: Increasing difficulty, or perfecting a musical piece or passage.

Props & Set Design:

- ✓ A chalkboard, or dry-erase board.

Story Board:

1. The goal of this activity is to practice increasingly-more challenging exercises, literature, and tempos.
2. This activity can be used for mastering one type of skill, while increasing the difficulty. Or the teacher may design it to include several different skills.
3. As in many video games, the player must master Level 1 before progressing to the next level. At the end of each level is an "enemy" that must be conquered. In addition, it usually takes several attempts before succeeding at each level. Typically the number of "lives"(attempts at each level) are limited, but many games provide opportunities to win more "lives."
4. Here is a sample game.
5. The skill is harmonization.

6. At each level you get three "lives." You may earn an extra life by playing the level with correct dynamics.
7. To complete each level, the student must play the exercise up to tempo, with most of the melody, and rhythm correct. All of the chords must be correct as well.

> Level 1: Simple melody, with simple chord progression, at a slow tempo – 4 measures long.
> Level 2: Simple melody, with simple chord progression, at a slow tempo – 8 measures long.
> Level 3: Simple melody, with simple chord progression, at a moderato tempo – 4 measures long.
> Level 4: Simple melody, with simple chord progression, at a moderato tempo – 8 measures long.
> Level 5: Simple melody, with medium chord progression, at a moderato tempo – 8 measures long.
> Level 7: Simple melody, with medium chord progression, at a quick tempo – 8 measures long.
> Level 8: Medium melody, with medium chord progression, at a quick tempo – 8 measures long.
> Level 9: Medium melody, with challenging chord progression, at a quick tempo – 8 measures long.
> Level 10: Complex melody, with challenging chord progression, at a quick tempo – 8 measures long.

Encore!!

The game can be more detailed, with opportunities to earn bonus points, or maybe even skip levels.

Don't Forget!!!

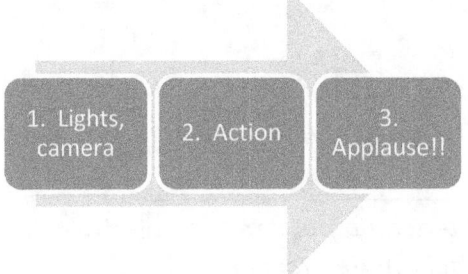

Important Plot Points

1. <u>Student Action</u> - "Playing" the piano version of a video game.

2. <u>Specific Feedback</u> You will need to listen closely during each level to make sure the player has played with accuracy, at the right tempo and with or without the correct dynamics. Explain to the student why s/he has or has not passed the level.

3. <u>Stunt Work</u> - Demonstrate some levels with varying accuracy so students have an idea of how they will be graded.

Behind the Scenes

1. **Action-packed.** As soon as a student passes a level, provide the exercise for the next level.

2. Costuming

3. Facial Expressions. Think Silent Films.

4. Sound System - Speak clearly.

5. Rehearsal. You may want to allow a few minutes to practice each level before the student attempts to pass it.

The Script:

> *The teacher will conduct several complete teaching patterns resembling the following script. They will follow this format:*
>
> 1. Ask students to play Level 2 with the correct dynamics.
>
> 2. Give time for student response.
>
> 3. Teacher Feedback =Explain why a student needs to attempt the level again. Was the tempo too slow? Was a chord played incorrectly? Were there missed notes in the melody?
>
>
> Teacher: "This next level has a more complex chord progression."
>
> Student Response = SR
>
> Teacher Feedback: "You'll need to try again. The chord in the third measure should be a D-major chord. The tempo also needs to be a little bit faster."

Game Five

Activity 5: Hurdles

Spotlight: Scales and arpeggios - speed and accuracy

Props & Set Design:

- ✓ Metronome

Story Board:

1. The goal of this activity is to become faster and more accurate when playing scales and arpeggios. Students are rewarded for faster tempos, accurate pitches, and correct fingerings.
2. In the track-and-field hurdles event, the winner of the race is not only the one who finishes with the fastest time, but also the one who did not bump or knock over any hurdles. The same concept applies to the piano hurdles event.
3. Students can compete in the 100 meter (one octave), 200 meter (two octaves), and 400 meter (4 octaves) events. Depending on the level of the class, the scales/arpeggios can either be hands-together or hands separate. Each student must pre-select his/her "pace" (tempo). Then play each student the scale/arpeggio, with the metronome, one student at a time.
4. The teacher watches each student to assess pitch accuracy and correct fingering. For inaccurate pitches and/or incorrect fingerings, a certain number of beats per second is

subtracted from the "pace." Therefore, it is not wise to choose a faster tempo than the student can handle.

    2 beats = only one or two incorrect pitches or fingering
    4 beats = about half of the pitches or fingerings are incorrect
    8 beats = the majority of the pitches or fingerings are incorrect.

5. The winner of the race is the one whose final metronome marking (number of beats per second) is the highest.

Don't Forget!!!

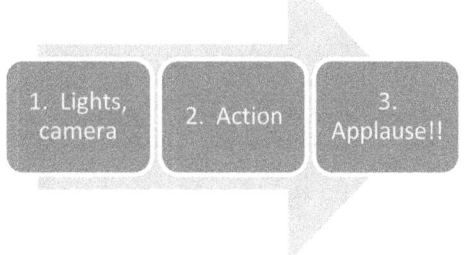

1. Student Action - Playing scales as fast and accurately as possible.	2. Specific Feedback If there are inaccuracies that result in a lower metronome marking, explain where they occurred.	3. Stunt Work - Demonstrate the fingerings for different scales/arpeggios, if necessary.

Important Plot Points

Games

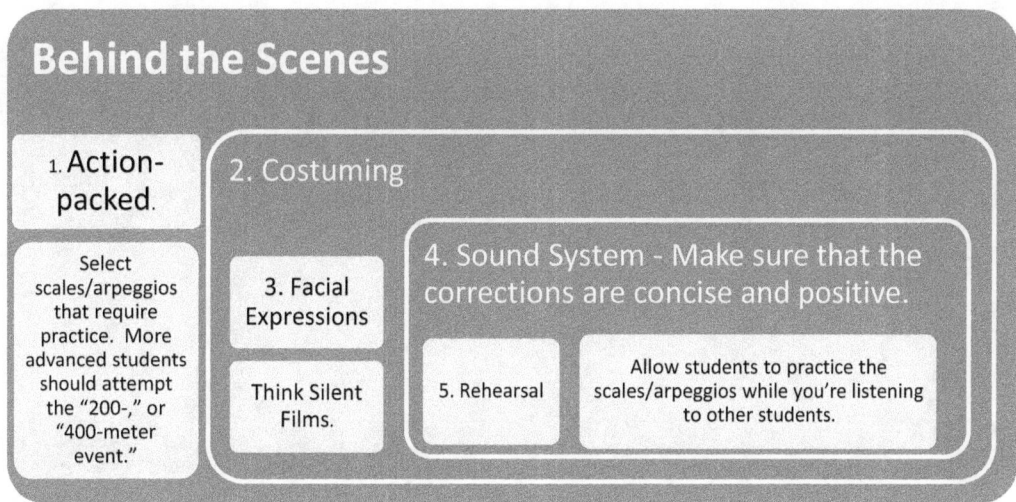

The Script:

> *The teacher will conduct several complete teaching patterns resembling the following script. They will follow this format:*
>
> 1. Ask the student to select a tempo for the scale, set the metronome, then play the scale or arpeggio.
>
> 2. Give time for student response.
>
> 3. Teacher Feedback = Point out incorrect fingering, inaccurate pitches, etc.
>
>
> Teacher: "Play the A scale, hands together, two octaves, and at 120 beats per minute."
>
> Student Response = SR
>
> Teacher Feedback: "Your left-hand fingering should have been, 5-4-3-2-1-3-2-1-4-3-2-1-3-2-1."

Game Six

Activity 6: Musical Pursuit

Spotlight: Harmonization, sight-reading, repertoire, technique, transposition, and improvisation

Props & Set Design:

- ✓ Enough Trivial Pursuit™ game-boards and game pieces to allow each student in the class to play as an individual.

Story Board:

1. The goal of this activity is to review skills, musical exercises, and musical pieces that students have studied throughout the class.
2. This game is played like the Trivial Pursuit™ game, except the categories are changed to the musical skills addressed in group piano classes.
3. For example:
   Yellow = Harmonization
   Orange = Sight-reading
   Green = Repertoire
   Purple = Technique
   Red = Transposition
   Blue = Improvisation

4. Students compete to collect tokens from each category. Instead of answering trivia questions, players must perform musical examples or exercises that fall into each category. The player must perform the exercise or example at the level that would normally earn an "A" grade in the class. Appoint trustworthy students to help in determining correct answers.

Don't Forget!!!

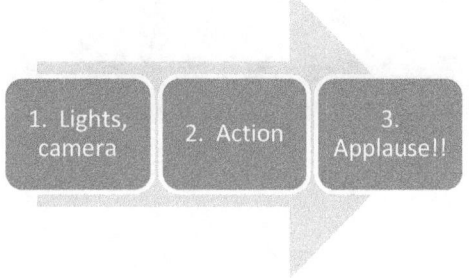

Important Plot Points

| 1. <u>Student Action</u> - Rolling the dice, drawing the cards, playing the musical excerpts, and collecting pie pieces. | 2. <u>Specific Feedback</u> If a student's answer is incorrect, explain what made his/her performance below "A-level." | 3. <u>Stunt Work</u> - Point out the locations for the cards, dice, and game pieces. Play musical excerpts, if necessary, to show how an incorrect answer should have been played. |

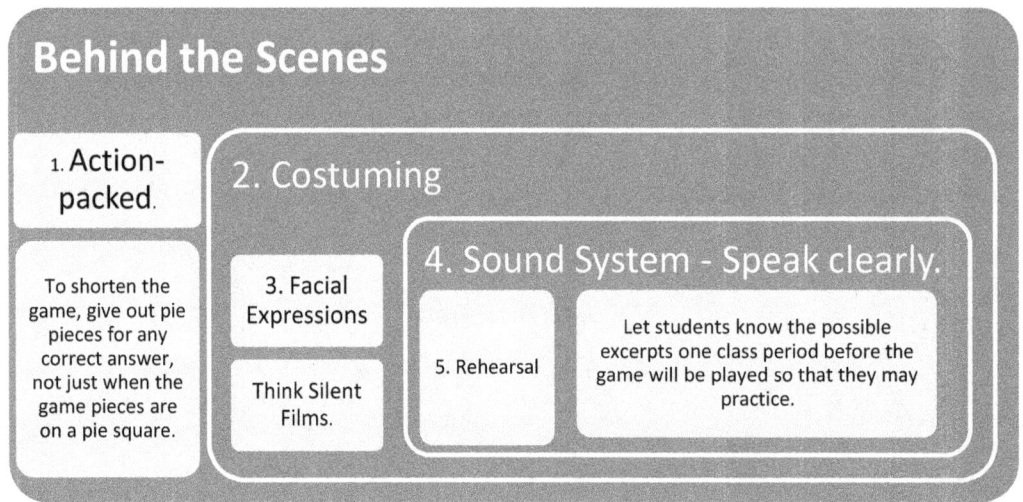

The Script:

The teacher will conduct several complete teaching patterns resembling the following script. They will follow this format:

1. Ask students to play the exercise of the card drawn.

2. Give time for student response.

3. Teacher Feedback = Explain why an incorrect answer is not correct.

Teacher: "The category is harmonization. Play exercise 2 on page 79."

Student Response = SR

Teacher Feedback: "The answer is incorrect. The chords in measures two and five should have been V7 chords.

Game Seven

Activity 7: Volleyball

Spotlight: Improvisation

Props & Set Design:

- ✓ Musical exercises that call for improvisation, or chord progressions with which an improvised melody may be added.

Story Board:

1. The goal of this activity is to improvise short segments without false starts or stopping altogether.
2. In volleyball, one team serves the ball to the other side. The opposing side then has three hits before the ball must be sent back over the net. If the opposing side lets the ball drop to the floor, or hits it more than three times before sending it back over the net, the serving team gets a point. If the opposing team is successful in hitting the ball over the net, the serving team has three hits before they must send the ball back to the opposing side. If the serving team lets the ball drop to the floor, or hits it more than three times before sending it back over the net, the opposing team does not get the point. Instead, the opposing team gets the opportunity to serve the ball, therefore becoming the serving team.
3. The musical improvisation version of this game is similar. The serving team "serves" by playing the first small section (two measures) of a larger improvisation exercise or chord

progression. The opposing team must then "hit" three times. This means that three players continue the exercise or chord progression, each by playing two measures at a time. These players must pick up their measures where the previous player left off, without any breaks in the music. S/he must also keep playing, regardless of mistakes. If one of the players on the opposing team allows a break in the music or stops before his/her measures are completed, it is considered a "drop." The serving team gets a point. If the members of the opposing team play their measures successfully, the serving team must continue the exercise or chord progression. They must pick up their measures where the opposing team (or the previous player) left off, without any breaks in the music. If one of the players on the serving team allows a break in the music, or stops before his/her measures are completed, it is considered a "drop." The opposing team gets the opportunity to serve, therefore becoming the serving team.
4. Servers only get one opportunity to serve. If s/he is unsuccessful, it is a "short serve." The opposing team then gets the opportunity to serve, therefore becoming the serving team.
5. Determine the order in which students will play their measures before the game begins. When the exercise or chord progression is passed to the other side of the net, students must remember who was the last person on their team to play part of the improvisation exercise. When it is passed back to their team, the next player in line will perform.
6. During one volley, the players continue to play the same exercise or chord progression. They should repeat it until a drop occurs. When a new team serves, they must change to a different exercise or chord progression.
7. The teacher is the line judge and has the power to determine whether or not a "drop" occurs.

Don't Forget!!!

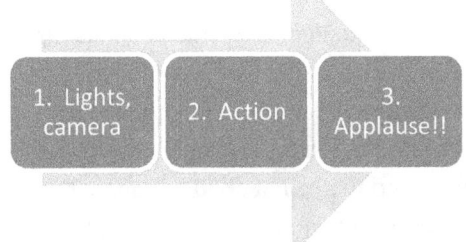

Important Plot Points

1. <u>Student Action</u> - Playing short segments of an improvisation exercise or chord progression.

2. <u>Specific Feedback</u> - Between volleys, recommend simple or new ideas for improvised melodies.

3. <u>Stunt Work</u> - Demonstrate possible melodic patterns for the improvisation exercises.

Behind the Scenes

1. **Action-packed**.

    Listening to, and performing improvisation exercises.

2. Costuming

    3. Facial Expressions

    Think Silent Films.

    4. Sound System - Call out line judge rulings clearly. Also, point to the side and/or person that must play next.

    5. Rehearsal

    Allow students to play the chord progressions and possible melodic motives before the game begins.

The Script:

> *The teacher will conduct several complete teaching patterns resembling the following script. They will follow this format:*
>
> 1. Ask students to play two measures of an improvisation exercise or chord progression.
>
> 2. Give time for student response.
>
> 3. Teacher Feedback = Explain why a certain performance is considered a "drop."
>
>
> Teacher: "Brad, it is your turn to serve."
>
> Student Response = SR
>
> Teacher Feedback: "The serving team gets a point because only two people on the opposing team continued the improvisation exercise."

Game Eight

Activity 8: Stress Ball Pass

Spotlight: Balancing tension and relaxation in the arms and shoulders.

When playing golf, the harder one tries, the worse s/he becomes. It is often the same case in piano. If a pianist tries harder by tensing his/her muscles, the result is usually the opposite of what is intended.

Props & Set Design:

- ✓ Tennis balls - One for each group of students
- ✓ Stress-relief balls (the kind you squeeze) - one for each group
- ✓ Stopwatch - one for each group
  Piano pieces that have fast passages.

Story Board:

1. The goal of this activity is to feel the difference between performing with too much tension, and using the right amount of tension.
2. Divide the class into two or three groups of equal number. The members of each group stand side by side. The groups race to pass a ball from one member to next, until it reaches the other side of the group. The first two races are done with the stress-relief balls. The group member furthest to the right takes the ball in his/her right hand and squeezes it while passing it to the person to the left. The next person takes the ball with

the right hand and squeezes it while passing the ball to the next person. Each group member uses only one hand to pass the ball. The first group to get the ball to the other end wins. To get a more accurate time, use the stopwatch.
3. Students will probably discover that they can go faster if they do not squeeze the ball as hard. To emphasize this concept, do the next two races with tennis balls. The races are the same, except that the students do not need to squeeze the tennis balls. They will just pass them. The times should be faster for these races.

Encore!!

Play piano pieces that have fast passages, remembering that extremely tense muscles will make the passages slower.

Don't Forget!!!

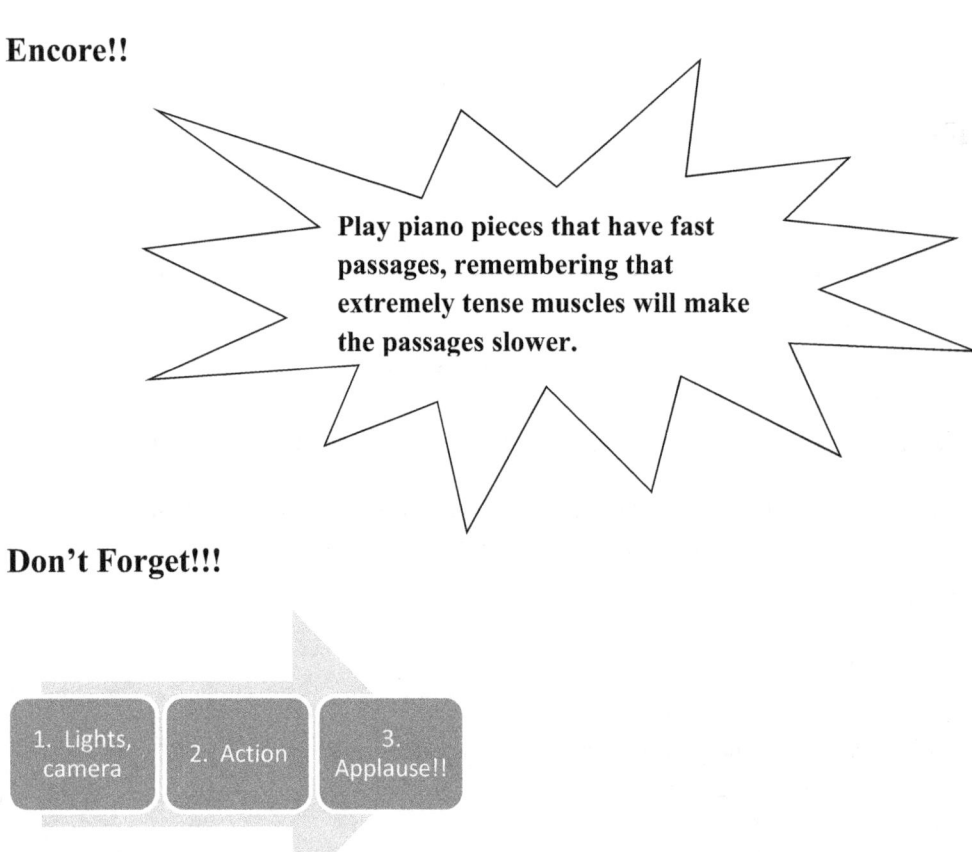

1. Lights, camera
2. Action
3. Applause!!

Important Plot Points

1. <u>Student Action</u> - Doing the ball-pass race.

2. <u>Specific Feedback</u> - When using the stress-relief balls, remind the students that they must squeeze the balls as they pass them.

3. <u>Stunt Work</u> - Demonstrate passing the ball.

Behind the Scenes

1. **Action-packed**.

   Do not let a lot of time lapse between races. Have the tennis balls nearby to make the switch quickly.

2. Costuming

   3. Facial Expressions

   Think Silent Films.

   4. Sound System - Explain the passing action while you demonstrate it. that must play next.

   5. Rehearsal

   Practice the passing action once without racing.

The Script:

> *The teacher will conduct several complete teaching patterns resembling the following script. They will follow this format:*
>
> 1. Ask students to squeeze the stress-relief ball and pass it as quickly as possible.
>
> 2. Give time for student response.
>
> 3. Teacher Feedback = Do not let students forget to squeeze the ball.
>
>
> Teacher: "This race is with tennis balls. Do not squeeze, but just pass the ball."
>
> Student Response = SR
>
> Teacher Feedback: "Notice that the times were faster since you did not need to squeeze."

Game Nine

Activity 9: Four Corners

Spotlight: Matching key signatures to the major and minor keys.

Props & Set Design:

- ✓ Slips of paper or cards each containing one major or minor key.
- ✓ A hat or a bowl to hold the key cards/papers.

Story Board:

1. The goal of the game is to be the last person standing.
2. Number the corners of the room, one through four.
   Corner 1 = 1 flat or 1 sharp (F major, D minor, G major, and E minor)
   Corner 2 = 2 flats or 2 sharps (B-flat major, G minor, D major, or B minor)
   Corner 3 = 3 flats or 3 sharps (E-flat major, C minor, A major, and F-sharp minor)
   Corner 4 = 4 flats or 4 sharps (A-flat major, F minor, E major, and C-sharp minor)
3. While music is playing, the students walk around the room. When the music stops, they should go to any corner. Once all students have chosen a corner, draw a key card/paper from the hat or bowl. The key that is drawn should correspond to one of the corners. The students standing in the corresponding corner are out for this round and must take a seat.
4. The game continues until only one student is standing.

Re-makes:

You can assign different key signatures to the corners, depending on the focus of the lesson or unit.

Encore!!

Play the blues scale in multiple keys, or a repertoire piece that utilizes the blues scale.

Don't Forget!!!

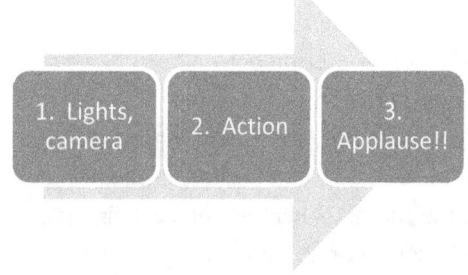

1. Lights, camera
2. Action
3. Applause!!

Games

Important Plot Points

1. Student Action
Tossing the rock and hopping on the hopscotch board.

2. Specific Feedback
Monitor the landings of each hop. Be sure the landing is on one foot when there are half steps.

3. Stunt Work - Show students how to hop on each section of the board, and how to toss the rock.

Behind the Scenes

1. Action-packed.
Encourage students to pass the rock quickly to the next person in line.

The activity will go faster by dividing the class and playing on multiple boards.

2. Costuming - Wear clothes that accommodate an activity that requires hopping.

3. Facial Expressions
Think Silent Films.

4. Sound System

5. Rehearsal — Allow students one or two practice tosses and hops.

Page 39

The Script:

> *The teacher will conduct several complete teaching patterns resembling the following script. They will follow this format:*
>
> 1. Tell the next student in line to toss the rock into the box labeled "5-flat."
>
> 2. Give time for student response.
>
> 3. Teacher Feedback = Since the rock didn't land inside the box, you will have to try again during your next turn.
>
>
> Teacher: "Now that you've tossed the rock, hop to that block. Make sure you land on one foot."
>
> Student Response = SR
>
> Teacher Feedback: "Not quite. You got to the right spot, but you forgot to land on one foot. This is a half step."

Game Ten

Activity 10: Blues Scale Hopscotch

Spotlight: Identifying the intervals that make up the blues scale.

Props & Set Design:
- A rock or something to toss onto the hopscotch board.
- Sidewalk chalk to draw a drawing of, or a mat with a drawing of the following hopscotch board.
- The hopscotch board is made up of single blocks and double blocks, which are placed side-by-side. The first section is a double block. Second is a single block. Third is double. Fourth is double. Fifth, sixth, and seventh are singles. Eighth and ninth are doubles.
- Write "Start" on the first section. Center the word in the middle of the two blocks. The second section should remain empty.
  Third, write "3-flat."
  4th = "4"
  5th = "5-flat"
  6th = "5"
  7th should remain empty.
  8th = "7-flat."
  9th = "8"

Games

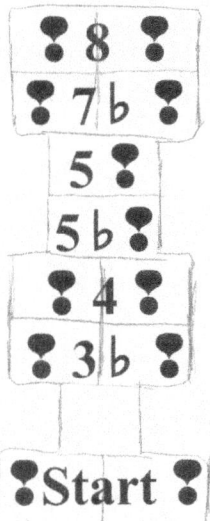

Story Board:

1. The goal of this activity is to practice the interval pattern that makes up a blues scale by playing hopscotch.
2. This hopscotch game is similar to regular playground hopscotch. There are some variations to go along with the blues scale.
3. Students still hop on one or two feet. Since the blues scale is made up of minor thirds, major seconds, and minor seconds, there are certain ways to hop that go with each interval.
   Minor third = hop over one section, landing on both feet.
   Major second = hop to the next section, landing on both feet.
   Minor second - hop to the next section, landing on one foot.
4. The labels on the hopscotch board correspond to the blues scale. The student must start on the first section, labeled "start." Then the student must hop over Section two, and land on Section three, labeled "3-flat." Since the first interval in a blues scale is a minor third, the student must land on two feet. Then s/he should jump from to the fourth section, labeled "4." Once again, s/he must land on both feet since the next interval is a major second. No one is allowed to land on the unlabeled blocks. These are in place to create large leaps for the minor thirds.
5. Students take turns tossing the rock onto the hopscotch board. For the first turn, toss the rock to the section labeled "3-flat." Then hop to that section, pick up the rock, then hop back to "Start." Hand the rock to the next student for his/her first turn.

Games

6. For the second turn, toss the rock to the section labeled "4." Hop to that section. Pick up the rock. Then hop back to "Start." Hand the rock to the next person.
7. For each successive turn toss the rock to the next section. If the rock does not land in the required section when tossed, the student loses a turn and must try for the same section on the next turn. The goal is to complete the hopscotch board. Whoever gets to the end first is the winner.

Re-makes:

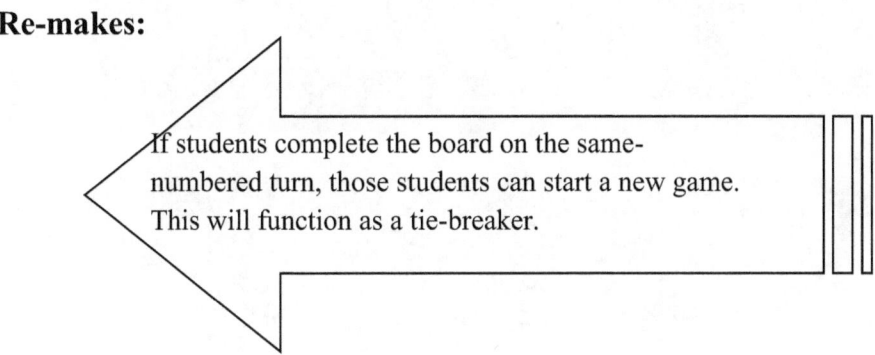

If students complete the board on the same-numbered turn, those students can start a new game. This will function as a tie-breaker.

Don't Forget!!!

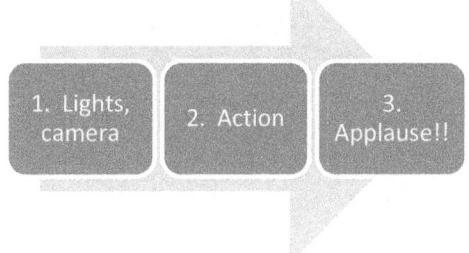

1. Lights, camera   2. Action   3. Applause!!

Important Plot Points

1. Student Action - Walking around the room, then sitting at the appropriate time.

2. Specific Feedback - Make sure students match the right key signatures to the keys drawn.

3. Stunt Work - Point to the individual corners when assigning the key signatures.

Behind the Scenes

1. **Action-packed.** Don't leave the music playing more than 10 or 15 seconds.

2. **Costuming**

3. **Facial Expressions** Think Silent Films.

4. **Sound System** - Speak clearly when assigning keys signatures to the corners, or calling out keys.

5. **Rehearsal** Do one practice round to clarify the rules. At the end of the round no students will have to sit down.

The Script:

The teacher will conduct several complete teaching patterns resembling the following script. They will follow this format:

1. Tell the students to go to any corner when the music stops.

2. Give time for student response.

3. Teacher Feedback = The game works better when students are spread somewhat evenly among the four corners.

Teacher: "The card says A major. "

Student Response = SR

Teacher Feedback: "Only the people in Corner 3 have to take a seat. Everyone else is still in the game."

The exercise continues adding more colors gradually to provide an appropriate challenge.

Game Eleven

Activity 11: Scale Fingering Dominoes

Spotlight: Identifying the two-hand fingerings of various scales.

Props & Set Design:

- ✓ Domino blocks, or cards resembling dominoes. Each domino must contain the number of dots for the left-hand finger number on one half and the number of dots for the right-hand finger number on the other half. [See diagram.]
- ✓ For example:
- ✓ Dominoes for the C major scale should have the following combinations:
- ✓ LH 5-RH 1, LH 4-RH 2, LH 3-RH 3, LH 2-RH 1, LH 1-RH 2, LH 3-RH 3, LH 2-RH 4, LH 1-RH 5.

Story Board:

1. The goal of this activity is to practice the fingerings of scales (hands together) by placing dominoes representing the finger numbers in order.
2. This activity works best as a drill. Unlike regular dominoes, the goal is not to connect same-numbered dominoes. Instead, the goal is to line up the dominoes containing the fingerings for specific scales in the right order, from *left* to *right*.

Games

3. The dominoes are laid flat on the table. They are positioned vertically (*North* to *South*), with the left-hand finger number on the bottom, and right-hand number on the top.

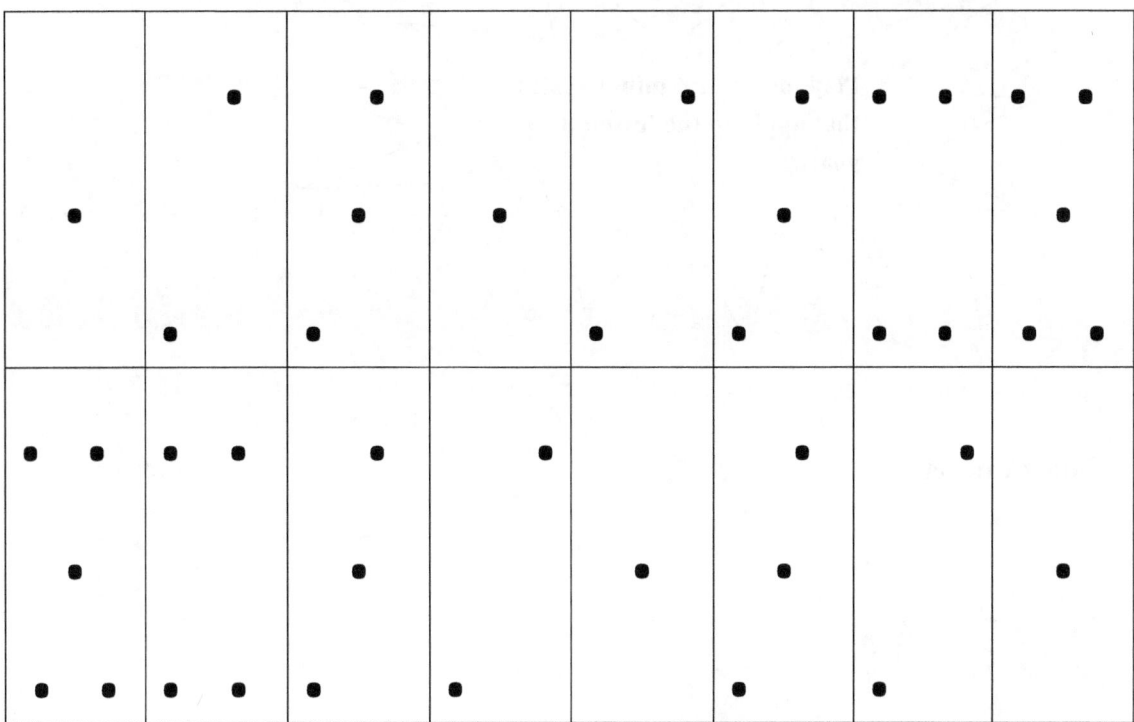

4. Students race against each other or individual times to create the fingerings.

Re-makes:

This activity will work for major and all types of minor scales.

Encore!!

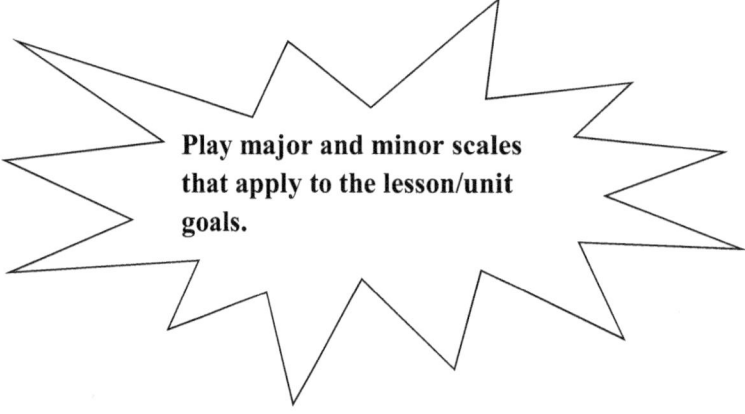

Don't Forget!!!

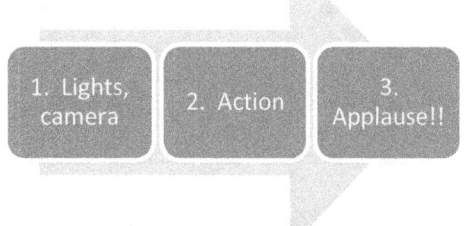

Important Plot Points

| 1. Student Action Placing the dominoes in the correct order. | 2. Specific Feedback Correct fingering mistakes. Be sure the left-hand number is on the bottom. | 3. Stunt Work - Place dominoes in the correct order as a sample. |

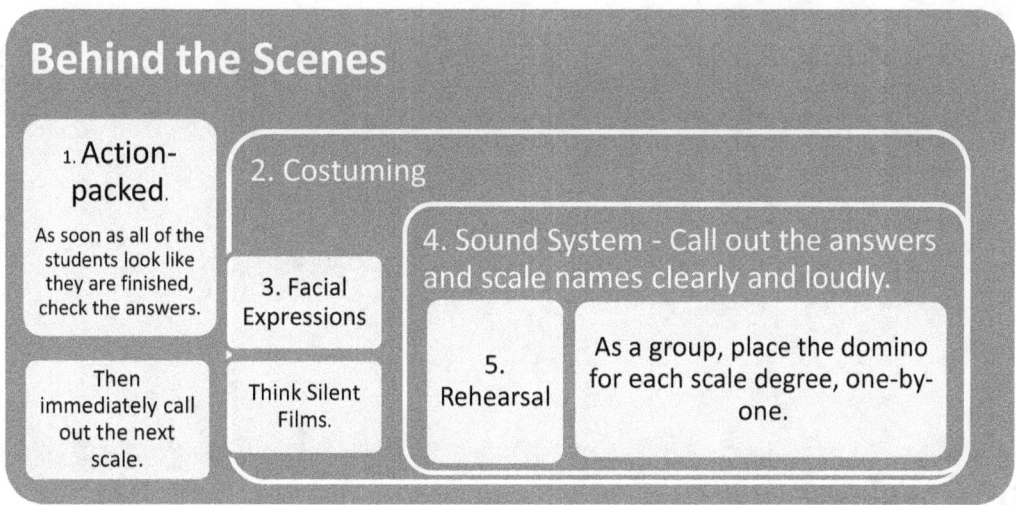

The Script:

> *The teacher will conduct several complete teaching patterns resembling the following script. They will follow this format:*
>
> 1. Ask students to create the C major scale fingering.
>
> 2. Give time for student response.
>
> 3. Teacher Feedback = Correct any fingering mistakes.
>
> Teacher: "Find the domino for the third degree of our practice scale."
>
> Student Response = SR
>
> Teacher Feedback: "That's right. The third domino should have a three on the bottom and a three on the top."

Game Twelve

Activity 12: Piano Telephone

Spotlight: Melodic Dictation; Playing a tune by ear.

Props & Set Design:

- ✓ One keyboard/piano placed in a separate area or room from the normal classroom.

Story Board:

1. The goal of this activity is to practice learning a tune by rote, using the traditional game of Telephone.
2. This game is played similarly to the traditional game of Telephone. One person starts a musical "message" that is passed from person to person until the final person plays the message for the group. The goal is to pass the musical message as accurately as possible so that the final recipient of the message will hear it played just as the first recipient heard it.
3. The teacher should be the first person to send a message. Create a short musical motive (something that will not be too difficult to reproduce "by ear."). The teacher plays the motive for the first student. The student/receiver is not allowed to watch the teacher play the motive. The student may only listen. The teacher may play the motive up to three times for the student/receiver and tell him/her the starting pitch.

4. Next, that student (Number 1) is allowed a few seconds to try to recreate the motive. The teacher may not help the student. The student must do his/her best to play the motive by ear. Once Student Number 1 has practiced for a moment, s/he becomes the next person to send the message. Student 2 becomes the new receiver.
5. Student 1 plays the motive for Student 2. The receiver (Student 2) is not allowed to watch Student 1 play the motive. Student 2 may only listen. Student 1 may play the motive up to three times for the receiver and tell him/her the starting pitch.
6. Next, Student 2 is allowed a few seconds to try to recreate the motive. Student 1 may not help Student 2. The Student 2 must do his/her best to play the motive by ear. Once Student Number 2 has practiced for a moment, s/he becomes the next person to send the message. Student 3 becomes the new receiver.
7. Continue in this fashion until all have heard the motive. The final receiver then plays the motive.
8. Finally, the teacher plays the original motive to see if it has changed throughout the process.

Re-makes:

This game can also be played to reinforce harmonic dictation by playing chord progressions rather than melodic motives.

Don't Forget!!!

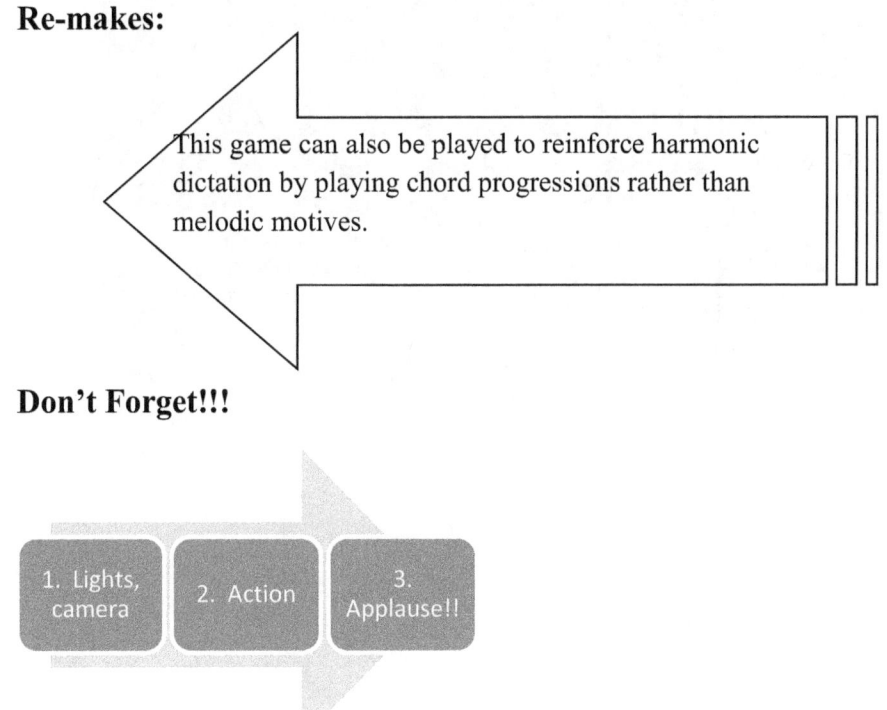

1. Lights, camera   2. Action   3. Applause!!

Important Plot Points

1. Student Action
Practicing and playing the melody.

2. Specific Feedback
Explaining the differences, in the rhythm and pitches, between the first and final motives.

3. Stunt Work
Playing the original melodic motive.

Behind the Scenes

1. Action-packed.
To prevent wasting class time, students who are waiting can be working on other lesson exercises.

2. Costuming

3. Facial Expressions
Think Silent Films.

4. Sound System - Be sure that the melodic motive is easy to hear, without outside noises to make things confusing.

5. Rehearsal
Start with simple, one-measure melodies.

Gradually extend the length of the melodies, according to the students' abilities.

The Script:

> *The teacher will conduct several complete teaching patterns resembling the following script. They will follow this format:*
>
> 1. Ask students to listen carefully to the melody and to then try to play it on their individual keyboards.
>
> 2. Give time for student response.
>
> 3. Teacher Feedback = Remind them to play the melody with the correct rhythm as well as the correct pitches.
>
> It is helpful to practice recreating one or two melodies as a class before passing a motive from one person to another.
>
> Teacher: "After I play this melody three times, practice playing the melody based on what you hear."
>
> Student Response = SR
>
> Teacher Feedback: (For this activity, feedback will be withheld until the final "receiver" plays the melodic motive. Then, when the teacher plays the original motive, students will hear the differences. The teacher will also describe the rhythmic and melodic differences.) "The first note should have been a half note, followed by descending eighths beginning on G."

Game Thirteen

Activity 13: Cross-training

Spotlight: Making the most of practice time by focusing on a certain skill for a short period of time.

Props & Set Design:

- ✓ Signs to post at each "station" to indicate which exercise to perform. These signs can be as simple as a piece of notebook paper taped to a wall, or as elaborate as an intricately-decorated poster. The stations will represent harmonization, technique, sight-reading, etc.
- ✓ Stopwatch
- ✓ Referee's whistle

Story Board:

1. The goal of this activity is to improve efficiency in practice by using a cross-training theme.
2. Students rotate through different stations which emphasize different piano skills. Only allow two to five minutes at each station. Specific goals for each station should be explained to the students prior to beginning the first station.
3. For example:

Games

4. At the Harmonization Station, the goal may be to play the first four measures of a harmonization exercise, hands together and with the designated accompaniment pattern.
5. If applicable review the practice steps that students can use to achieve each goal more quickly.
6. For example:
7. At the Sight-reading Station
   1. Practice tapping the rhythm alone
   2. Look for unusual or challenging intervals
   3. Look for places where the hand must move.
8. Place a few students at each station after the stations have been explained. Start the stopwatch. At the conclusion of the two to five minutes, blow the whistle. This indicates that it is time to rotate to the next station. Reset the stopwatch for the second rotation.
9. Continue until all students have done the exercises at every station.

Re-makes:

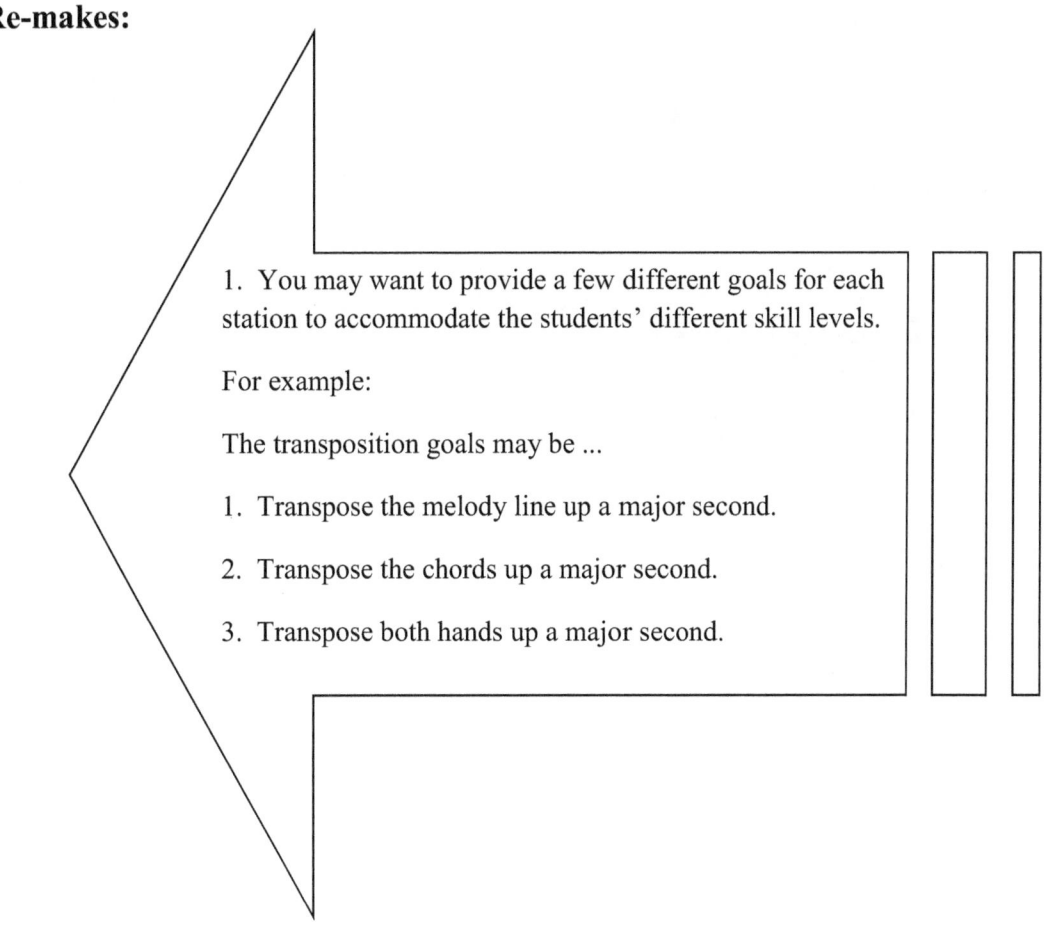

1. You may want to provide a few different goals for each station to accommodate the students' different skill levels.

For example:

The transposition goals may be ...

1. Transpose the melody line up a major second.

2. Transpose the chords up a major second.

3. Transpose both hands up a major second.

2. Each station can be a smaller section of a larger work, rather than different separate piano skills. This way, students are required to focus on only one section at a time.

Don't Forget!!!

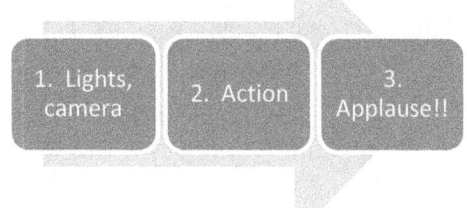

Important Plot Points

1. Student Action — Rotating from one station to another.

2. Specific Feedback — Listen to various students at the different stations and correct practice techniques, etc.

3. Stunt Work — Blow the referee's whistle. Start, stop and restart the stopwatch.

Behind the Scenes

1. **Action-packed.** Limiting the amount of time at each station should keep things moving quickly.

2. **Costuming**
   - 3. **Facial Expressions** — Think Silent Films.
   - 4. **Sound System**
     - 5. **Rehearsal** — Review specific practice steps for the different kinds of piano skills.

The Script:

> *The teacher will conduct several complete teaching patterns resembling the following script. They will follow this format:*
>
> 1. Ask students to practice the designated exercises or musical excerpts at their current stations.
>
> 2. Give time for student response.
>
> 3. Teacher Feedback = Remind them of specific steps that are effective in practicing the given exercise.
>
>
> Teacher: "You are already seated at a station. Look at t sign hanging close to your keyboard. Practice the skill for that station. I will blow the whistle at the end of 3 minutes. Then rotate clockwise to the next station."
>
> Student Response = SR
>
> Teacher Feedback: "You will be more productive if you work on this section first. Then you can go to the next step."

Credits:

> The idea for this activity was inspired by *Ready-to-use motor skills & movement station lesson plans for young children,* written by J. M. Landy & K. R. Burridge (2000).

Game Fourteen

Activity 14: I Write the Songs

Spotlight: Composition and learning by rote.

Props & Set Design:

- ✓ A piano.

Story Board:

1. The goal of this activity is to try to compose a melody or song, one measure at a time, and then to learn the new composition by rote, one measure at a time.
2. The activity follows the same format as the traditional game that begins, "I'm going to grandma's house, and I'm bringing ...(my coat)." The next person says, "I'm going to grandma's house, and I'm bringing my coat, and ...(my doll)." Each person takes a turn, adding to the list of items to be brought. The goal of the game is to remember each item, in order. If someone says one of the items out of order, s/he is out. The game continues until only one person is left.
3. This activity is played in the same manner, except each person composes a measure of the melody or song instead of listing an item. The next person plays the previously composed measure(s) in the correct order, then adds a new measure to the composition.

If someone plays the measures out of order, or forgets part of the composition, s/he is out. The activity continues until only one person is left.
4. This activity can be as basic, or as complicated as necessary. For instance, you may limit the melody to only whole notes within a major five-finger pattern. This means that each student will only at one (whole) note at a time.
5. To make it more complicated, allow students to use shorter note-lengths (sixteenth, eighth, quarter, and half notes) within the measures so that they may use more than one pitch. You may also extend the range to a full one-octave scale, or ask students to add a left-hand chord with the right-hand melody.
6. Use your discretion when determining the complication parameters for your class.

Re-makes:

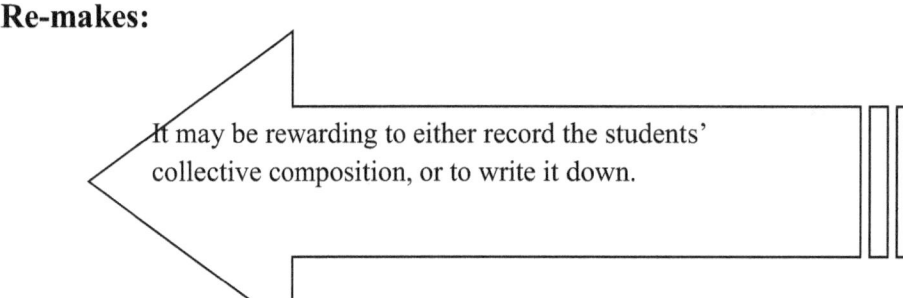

It may be rewarding to either record the students' collective composition, or to write it down.

Don't Forget!!!

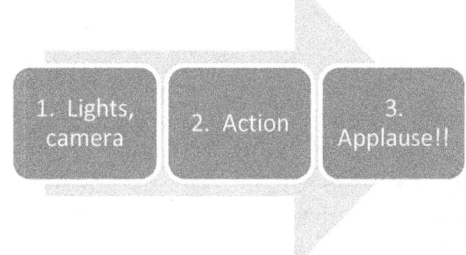

1. Lights, camera
2. Action
3. Applause!!

Important Plot Points

1. **Student Action** — Composing, memorizing, and playing the composition.

2. **Specific Feedback** — Explaining specific parameters for the composition.

3. **Stunt Work** — Demonstrate sample measures for composition. Play the first measure of the composition.

Behind the Scenes

1. **Action-packed.** Students will need to pay close attention to each new measure that is composed so that s/he can play it on his/her turn.

2. **Costuming**

3. **Facial Expressions** Think Silent Films.

4. **Sound System** - You can discuss the parameters of the composition as you demonstrate sample measures.

5. **Rehearsal** - - Begin with simplicity for the first composition. Then change to slightly more complex possibilities.

The Script:

> *The teacher will conduct several complete teaching patterns resembling the following script. They will follow this format:*
>
> 1. Ask students to play the already composed measures, then add a new measure (within the parameters.).
>
> 2. Give time for student response.
>
> 3. Teacher Feedback =Correct any notes not included in the given range. Let students know if the composition has been altered.
>
>
> Teacher: "Susan, you must now play measures *one* through *three*, then compose measure four."
>
> Student Response = SR
>
>
> Teacher Feedback: "F natural is not part of the D major five-finger pattern. Please alter your new measure to change the F natural."

Game Fifteen

Activity 15: The Gambler

Spotlight: Improvisation of a melody, given a specific rhythm.

Props & Set Design:

- ✓ A pair of dice with varying rhythmic motives on each side.
- ✓ The dice can be made by covering children's building blocks with pieces of paper that contain different rhythms. Each rhythm should be the length of one measure. When the two dice are rolled, the rhythms will combine to make up two measures..

Story Board:

1. The goal of this activity is to utilize specific rhythmic motives to improvise a melody.
2. Students can be given individual assignments, or may be divided into small groups. In small groups, each person takes turns rolling the dice and creating a melody. To begin, keep the exercise simple.
3. The first student rolls the dice, displaying two measures of rhythm. The student decides which order to play the rhythms. After a minute or two, s/he must play a two-measure melody using the rhythms that were rolled by the dice. The dice are then passed to the next person in the group. Continue until everyone has had a turn.

4. During the following rounds, increase the complexity by gradually extending the lengths of the melodies. This can be done by re-rolling the dice, or allowing students to create their own rhythms for extra measures. .

Re-makes:

Perform the activity by giving the students individual assignments. Pass the dice around the room, allowing each student to roll. Allow the entire class time to create short melodies that incorporate the rhythms that were rolled. Then have each student perform in a short recital-type format.

Don't Forget!!!

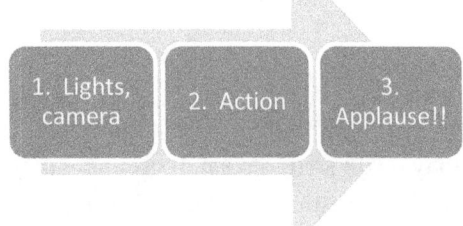

1. Lights, camera   2. Action   3. Applause!!

Games

Important Plot Points

1. Student Action
Rolling the dice, and performing the melodies.

2. Specific Feedback
Correcting rhythms that are incorrectly performed.

3. Stunt Work
Demonstrating how to roll the dice, determine the order of rhythms, and perform a melody.

Behind the Scenes

1. **Action-packed.**

Encourage students to play their melodies almost immediately to truly be improvising.

2. **Costuming**

3. **Facial Expressions**

Think Silent Films.

4. **Sound System**

5. Rehearsal

Begin with two-measure melodies that remain within five-finger major and minor patterns.

The Script:

> *The teacher will conduct several complete teaching patterns resembling the following script. They will follow this format:*
>
> 1. Ask students to play a melody after rolling the dice.
>
> 2. Give time for student response.
>
> 3. Teacher Feedback =Correcting incorrect rhythms.
>
>
> Teacher: "Keep your melody within the A-major five-finger pattern."
>
> Student Response = SR
>
> Teacher Feedback: "Don't forget to keep a steady beat."

Credits:

> The idea for this activity was inspired by *Summer smarts for cool kids: Over 150 fantastic and fun learning activities to help kids beat the summer blahs*, written by P. Warner (2002).

Game Sixteen

Activity 16: Charade (Sort of)

Spotlight: Performing and listening for variations of character in piano pieces.

Props & Set Design:

- ✓ A list of descriptors that pertain to the way a piano piece may be played. For example:
- ✓ Sleepy, melancholy, excited, bouncy, heavy, light, jazzy, etc.
- ✓ Slips of paper, each with one of the descriptors, placed into a hat (or box).
- ✓ Musical excerpts that may be performed in varying styles (to match the descriptors.). The excerpts should be easy for the students, or ones that the students have already practiced so that they do not stumble over notes or rhythms.

Story Board:

1. The goal of this activity is to encourage the students to play pieces musically and to listen for musicality in others' piano performances.
2. Students each draw a slip of paper from the hat. Students take turns performing the musical excerpt to represent the descriptor that was drawn. The other students listen

while one student is performing. They must look through the list of the descriptors and try to select the one that the performing student has drawn from the hat.
3. It is alright if some of the descriptors in the hat are duplicates. This prevents the "process of elimination" approach to selecting a descriptor off of the list.

Don't Forget!!!

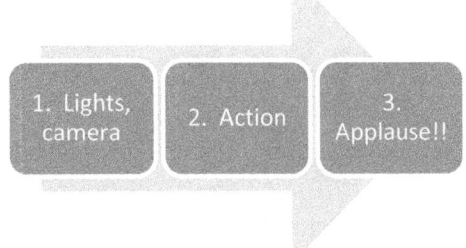

Important Plot Points

1. <u>Student Action</u>
Drawing slips of paper from the hat and performing the musical excerpts.

2. <u>Specific Feedback</u>
Tell students to exaggerate their performances in order to help the others figure out the descriptor.

3. <u>Stunt Work</u>
Perform some musical excerpts in a few different characters.

Behind the Scenes

1. Action-packed.

2. Costuming

Students should shout out the possible descriptor, just like the traditional charades game.

3. Facial Expressions

4. Sound System

Think Silent Films.

5. Rehearsal

While you are demonstrating, tell students to look at the list and try to find the descriptor you are using.

The Script:

> *The teacher will conduct several complete teaching patterns resembling the following script. They will follow this format:*
>
> 1. Ask students to play the excerpt according to the descriptor that was drawn.
>
> 2. Give time for student response.
>
> 3. Teacher Feedback =Discuss why the music sounds jazzy, bouncy, sleepy, etc.
>
>
> Teacher: "Jason, it is your turn to play your excerpt."
>
> Student Response = SR
>
> Teacher Feedback: "It is difficult to hear a different character. Try to exaggerate the descriptor."

Credits:

> The idea for this activity was inspired by *Games with books: 28 of the best children's books and how to use them to help your child learn – from preschool to third grade*, written by P. Kaye (2002).

Game Seventeen

Activity 17: Chord Progression Scrabble

Spotlight: Roots of chords of designated chord progressions (I-V-I; I-IV-I; etc.)

Props & Set Design:

- ✓ A game board resembling a scrabble board. A scrabble board may work. Squares should indicate whether points should be doubled, tripled, etc.
- ✓ Game pieces resembling scrabble pieces. The pieces should contain names of pitches – one pitch per game piece. Each game piece should contain a small number indicating the points value.
- ✓ Easel to display each player's game pieces.

Story Board:

1. The goal of this activity to place the roots and/or bass notes of chord progressions in order on a scrabble board.
2. The game can be played by two or more players.
3. Place all game pieces face down on the table. Each player selects seven game pieces and places them on his/her easel.
4. One or more chord progressions are chosen prior to play (by the teacher). Each player attempts to place the game pieces representing the roots of the chords in a row or line on

the game board. The remaining players confirm the correctness of the roots of the chords. The total number of points is recorded for that player's turn.
5. The number of game pieces placed on the board are replaced by new, unused game pieces.
6. If the player cannot create one of the designated chord progressions from his/her game pieces, s/he must wait until her next turn to try again.
7. Each subsequent player must create a progression using at least one pitch already on the game board.

Re-makes:

Rather than playing only roots of chords, players may also play bass-line pitches of traditional chord progressions (e.g., C-B-C works for the I-V7-I progression in C major.).

Encore!!

Play musical examples that utilize the chord

Games

Don't Forget!!!

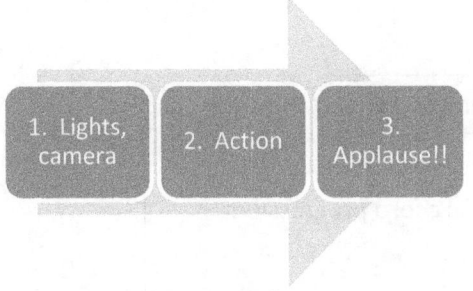

1. Lights, camera
2. Action
3. Applause!!

Important Plot Points

1. <u>Student Action</u> - Creating chord progressions on the Scrabble board

2. <u>Specific Feedback</u> - Correcting the chord progressions created.

3. <u>Stunt Work</u> - Place some examples of possible combinations players can use during the game.

Behind the Scenes

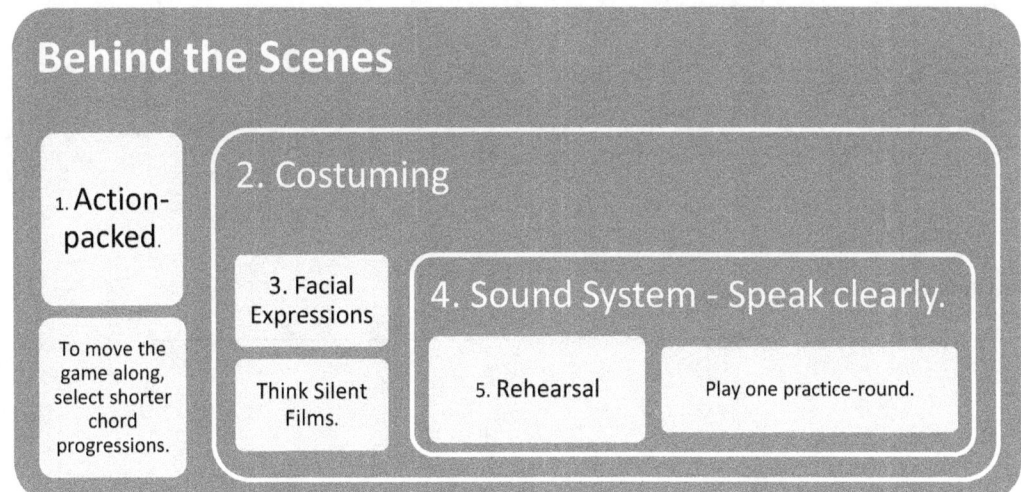

1. **Action-packed.**
   To move the game along, select shorter chord progressions.

2. **Costuming**

3. Facial Expressions
   Think Silent Films.

4. Sound System - Speak clearly.

5. Rehearsal — Play one practice-round.

The Script:

> The teacher will conduct several complete teaching patterns resembling the following script. They will follow this format:
>
> 1. Ask students to create the bass line for a specific chord progression
>
>   For example: I-V-I in D major is D-A-D
>
> 2. Give time for student response.
>
> 3. Teacher Feedback = Correcting incorrect pitches.
>
>
> Teacher: "Your goal is to create a bass line for a I-V-I chord progression. The bass line should be made up of the roots of each chord. If you have the pitches to create a bass line among your game pieces, you may play them on the game board."
>
> Student Response = SR
>
>
> Teacher Feedback: "Those pitches can work as a bass line for the I-V-I chord progression if we used chord inversions. For this round we are using roots of chords only. Change the middle pitch to an 'A.'"
>
>
> The game continues according to the rules.

Game Eighteen

Activity 18: Key Signature War

Spotlight: Identifying the key signatures for major and minor keys.

Props & Set Design:
- ✓ A deck of cards (52 is a good number) with either letter names of keys or key signatures. The keys can be either major or minor depending on the emphasis of the lesson.

Story Board:
1. The goal of this activity is to practice identifying relative major and minor keys along with their key signatures by playing a card game.
2. The game is played similarly to the playing-card game, "War."
3. It is a two-player game. Each player takes half of the deck of cards and places it down in front of him/her.
4. The players simultaneously take the top card off of each deck and place them face-up in between them. The player who played the higher card takes both of the cards and sets them to the side.
5. The high card is determined by drawing a card from the middle of the deck before it is divided for the two players. Whatever key is drawn represents the highest key for that game.

For example:
1. Before the game starts, the F key signature card is drawn. Therefore, F is the highest key for the game.
2. Player 1 plays a B card, while Player 2 plays a card with the key signature for E major. Since E is higher than B, Player 2 takes the cards.
3. If both players play a card representing the same key, they "war." Those cards remain where they are while each player plays one more card next to his/her first card. The player who plays the higher (2nd) card takes all four cards. If the second round produces two cards representing the same key, the "war" continues. Each player then plays one more card next to his/her second card. The player who plays the higher (3rd) card takes all six cards. The war continues until someone plays a higher card.
4. Once the players have played through their stacks, they start again with the card that have been set aside.
5. The game continues until one person has taken all of the cards in the deck, and the other player is left with no cards. The player with all the cards is the winner.

Don't Forget!!!

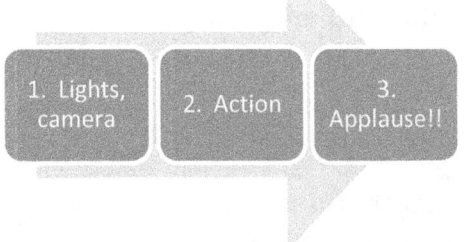

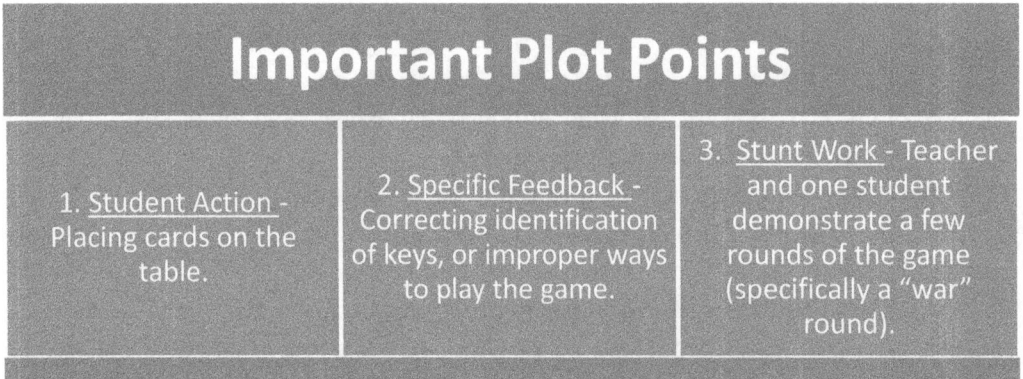

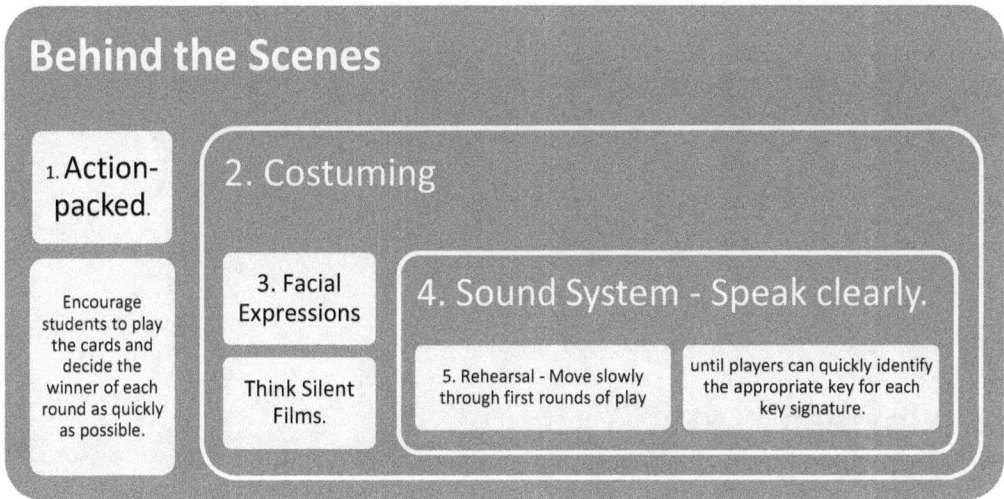

The Script:

The teacher will conduct several complete teaching patterns resembling the following script. They will follow this format:

1. Explain that A is higher than E if the "high key" is B, C, or D.

2. Give time for student response.

3. Teacher Feedback = Correct key signatures that incorrectly identified.

Teacher: "Players 1 and 2, take the top card off of each of your decks. Place those cards face-up in the middle of the table."

Student Response = SR

Teacher Presentation: "Good. Now decide whose key is higher."

Student Response = SR

Teacher Feedback: "Actually, Player 1's card is higher since A is higher than E. Remember that the High key is C."

Game Nineteen

Activity 19: Pentachord/Scale Game

Spotlight: Major Five-finger Patterns and Triads (Whole- and half-steps) of all keys

Props & Set Design:

- ✓ One set of game pieces includes five white notecards (blank, and of any size) and five black notecards. The number of sets needed depends on the game variation selected.
- ✓ Another game variation calls for seven white notecards, labeled: C, D, E, F, G, A, B for each white key on the piano. Five black note cards, labeled: C#/Db, D#/Eb, F#/Gb, G#/Ab, and A#/Bb, for each black key on the piano.
- ✓ Have a keyboard or image of a keyboard to demonstrate the half-steps, whole-steps, and major five-finger patterns. This way students can visualize each pattern.

Story Board:

1. The goal of this activity is to practice the white-key/black-key combination of different five-finger patterns and scales by placing black and white notecards in order.
2. The game is best played by the entire class. Each student should have a set of game pieces. Another option is to divide the class into three to five groups. Each group would have one set of game pieces in this scenario.

3. Each player (or group) is given five "black keys" and five "white keys." These can be made out of something as simple as index cards. You may also apply an adhesive like felt (for a felt board), velcro, or magnets in order to place the pieces up on a board. The students may also lay them out on a table or hold them up.
4. The goal is to arrange the black and white keys correctly to form the major five-finger pattern that the caller (the teacher or a student) calls out.
5. Example:
   D = white, white, black, white, white
6. It may be necessary to do a few practice rounds.
7. The students compete to see who can create the patterns the fastest. The leader of the group (or all of the students in the group) sits down to indicate that they have finished forming the pattern.
8. The teacher checks that the pattern is formed correctly. The first teach to form the pattern correctly gets a point. Once the patterns are created, remove the 2nd and 4th pitches to create the major triad.
9. Rotate through members of the groups. Player 1 of each group arranges the game pieces during the first round, then Player 2 plays the second round, and so on.
10. Another option is to pair stronger students with those who may not work as quickly. Each pair can function as an individual team.
11. The game continues until all of the major five-finger patterns have been covered at least once.

Re-makes:

1. Each person has his/her own set of game pieces and races against the rest of the class.

2. The black and white keys actually have pitch names on them, so students must also have the correct pitches in their major five-finger patterns.

3. Call out triads instead of five-finger patterns or mix them.

4. The game can also be played using minor five-finger patterns and triads, as well as major and minor scales.

In additional option is to have students play each pattern after it is created in the game.

If one student struggles with creating it, but can apply it to the piano, ask him/her to be the designated "performer" for the group. This way s/he is succeeding at pentascales too.

Encore!!

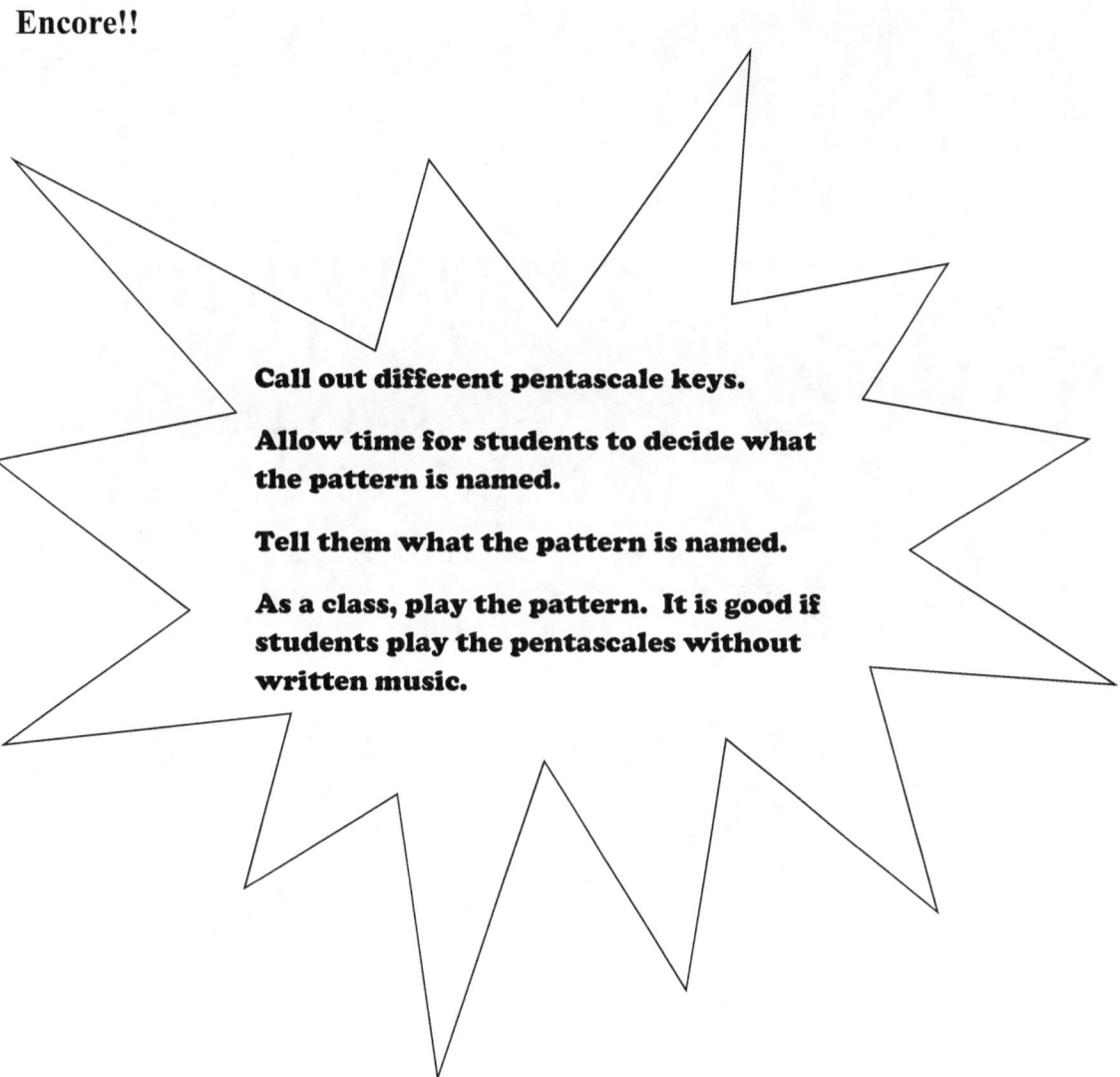

Call out different pentascale keys.

Allow time for students to decide what the pattern is named.

Tell them what the pattern is named.

As a class, play the pattern. It is good if students play the pentascales without written music.

Don't Forget!!!

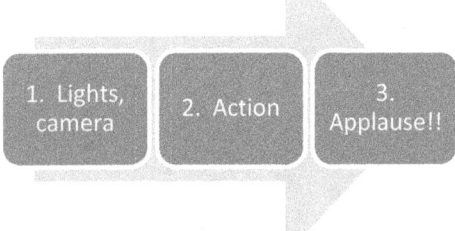

Important Plot Points

1. <u>Student Action</u> - Putting together the black-and-white card combinations.

2. <u>Specific Feedback</u> - (correcting the black-white pattern combinations) - Make sure to let everyone know the correct answer after each attempt.

3. <u>Stunt Work</u> - Demonstrate the different half-step/whole-step combinations.

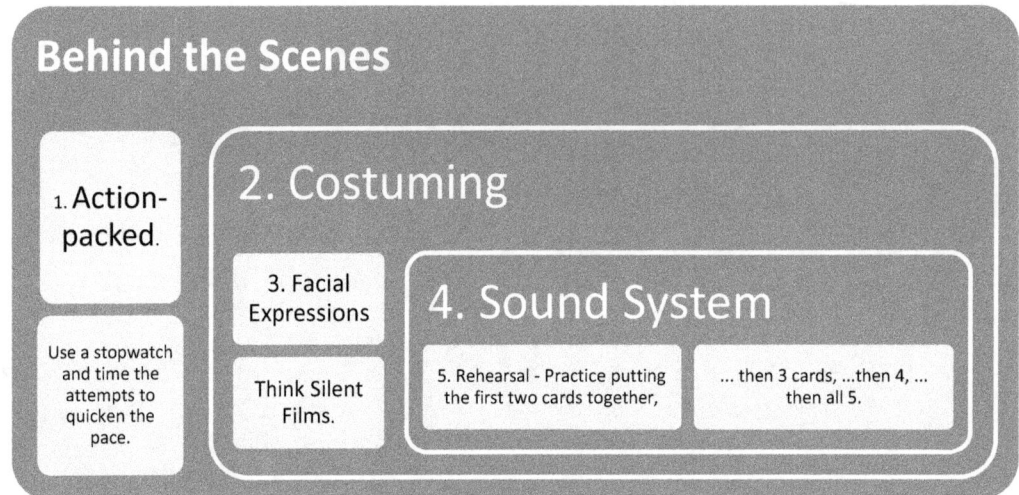

Page 82

The Script:

> The teacher will conduct several complete teaching patterns resembling the following script. They will follow this format:
>
> 1. Teacher calls out the combo
>
>   For example, "First 3 keys of D major."
>
> 2. Give time for student response.
>
> 3. Teacher Feedback = "The answer is 'white-white-black.'"
>
> Teacher: "Let's practice whole-steps (or half-steps, five-finger patterns/pentascales, etc.)."
>
> Student Response = SR
>
> Teacher Presentation: "For the next series of whole-steps, your starting key will be a white key. Place a white key/card on the table now. After I call out the starting key, place a card down that represents a whole-step up from the first key. It may be a white key, but it could also be a black key. Remember that E, up a whole-step is F#. So that will be white-to-black. It is the same for B. Up a whole-step is C#."
>
> "The first one is up a whole-step from C. Go!" (Drama! Drama! Drama!)
>
> Student Response (SR)
>
> Teacher Feedback: "You should have put a white key down, because a whole-step up from C is D, which is a white key. [Demonstrate on the keyboard image](illustrator/demonstrator in kinesics) Here is the C on the keyboard. To go up a whole step, you must skip this black key (C#/Db) and go to D."

Repeat the previous pattern for all of the white-to-white combos (D-E, F-G, G-A, and A-B).

Practice all 2-key patterns starting on a white key as follows:

Teacher Presentation: "The starting note is C. (then D, E, F, G, A, and B). Go!"

OR

Teacher Feedback: "The answer is D. (then E, F#, G, A, B, and C#)."

Repeat the process, starting on black keys.

Then repeat the process with a combination of 3 keys with the pattern Tonic-Whole-Whole).

    C-D-E

    D-E-F#

    E-F#-G#

    ... etc.

Then repeat the process with 4-key combinations (Tonic-Whole-Whole-Half).

Then repeat the process with 5-key combinations/pentascales (Tonic-Whole-Whole-Half-Whole).

It may be possible to start with the 3-, 4-, or 5-key combos, depending on the students' familiarity with pentascales/five-finger patterns.

Game Twenty

Activity 20: The Natural (A baseball game)

Spotlight: Review Skills, Pieces, and Musical Exercises

Props & Set Design:

- ✓ One six-sided die
- ✓ Selected piano skills, musical pieces/excerpts and musical exercises of the course's current unit.
- ✓ The piano skills, musical pieces/excerpts and musical exercises are to be divided into five different categories (four different difficulty levels). The length of some exercises may make them more difficult. A section of a repertoire piece may be selected to represent part of an easier level.
- ✓ Place the musical excerpts/pieces, skills, and exercises into the following categories:
    - o Bunt: The easiest level. Students will know specifically what these are ahead of their batting time so they can practice.
    - o Single: As easy as "Bunt," but not revealed until the student is at bat.
    - o Double: Slightly harder than "Bunt," and "Single." Not revealed until the student is at bat.
    - o Triple: Slightly harder than "Double." Not revealed until the student is at bat.
    - o Home Run: The most difficult level. Not revealed until the student is at bat.

Story Board:

1. The goal of this game is to review musical skills or excerpts by using a baseball format.
2. The rules of the game are very close to the rules of baseball. However, there are no defensive plays. Batters may only strike out. There are three strikes before striking out, and three outs before changing from defense to offense.
3. Divide the class into two teams. Have each team decide a batting order.
4. The first batter of the first team at bat comes "up to the plate," and rolls the die or chooses to bunt. If the batter bunts, s/he plays the next example from the "bunt" list. If the batter is successful, s/he advances one base. If the batter rolls the die instead, s/he must play whatever type of hit is rolled.
   a. 1 = Single - the player must play the next musical example on the "Single" list. If successful, all runners advance one base.
   b. 2 = Double - the player must play the next musical example on the "Double" list. If successful, all runners advance two bases.
   c. 3 = Triple - the player must play the next musical example on the "Triple" list. If successful, all runners advance three bases.
   d. 4 = Home Run - the player must play the next musical example on the "Home Run" list. If successful, all runners run home.
   e. 5 = a ball. roll again.
   f. 6 = a ball, roll again.
5. If four "balls" are rolled before another number is rolled, the student "walks" (advances) one base, along with all other runners.
6. The Umpire (teacher) has the last word on whether an attempt at a musical example is a strike or a hit.
7. A normal game lasts nine innings. Due to time constraints, it may be necessary to limit the innings to fewer than nine.

Re-makes:

To shorten the time of each inning, allow fewer strikes, or switch to defense at the end of the batting order.

Special Effects:

- *Use umpire signals*
- *Encourage cheering from the dugout.*

Don't Forget!!!

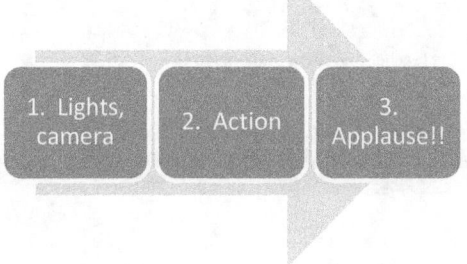

Important Plot Points

| 1. <u>Student Action</u> - Students will begin to anticipate the types of musical examples in each "hit" category. Encourage them to practice the exercises and pieces from their current units. | 2. <u>Specific Feedback</u> - (correcting the pitches, rhythms, dynamics, and tempo of each musical example. Be sure to explain exactly WHY a strike is a strike, if you call it that way.) - Make sure to let everyone know the corrections after each attempt. | 3. <u>Stunt Work</u> - You will need to play musical examples when explaining why an attempt was a "strike." |

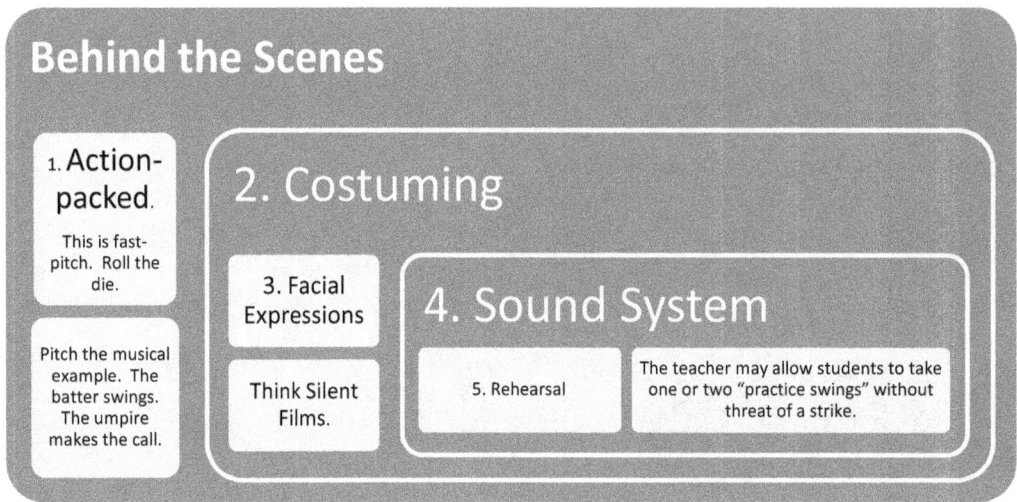

The Script:

The teacher will conduct several complete teaching patterns resembling the following script. They will follow this format:

1. Teacher "pitches the ball."

2. Give time for student response

3. Teacher Feedback = "Strike. The 'F' should have been an 'F#.'"

Teacher presentation: "The first batter rolls the die, or chooses to bunt. Remember a bunt means you can play one of the examples from this list. Which do you choose?"

SR: "I'll bunt."

Teacher Feedback: "Good, safe choice."

Teacher presentation: "Let me hear example # 1."

SR

Teacher feedback: "Right. Go to first."

Game Twenty One

Activity 21: Triad Bingo

Spotlight: Triads of Major Keys

Props & Set Design:

- ✓ Bingo cards with the names of different triads of major keys
- ✓ Bingo chips to cover the letters on the card
- ✓ A sample card can look like this:

M	m	d	m	M
G	E	C	A	F#
A	C	E	G	B
F	D	*	B	Ab
E	F	A	D	C#
C	D	E	F	G

- ✓ The letters in the top row are mandatory. They indicate the quality of the chord.
  - o M = Major
  - o m = Minor
  - o d = Diminished
- ✓ The middle space is a free space

1. **Story Board:**
2. The goal of this game is to practice building major triads by playing Bingo.
3. The game is similar to BINGO. The teacher calls out a letter and a number. The letter, in this game, indicates the major key to apply to the chord. The number indicates the scale degree that is the root of the triad or dominant-seventh chord.
4. If the teacher calls out "C - 2," the students are to cover a "D." "D" is the second degree ("2") of the C major scale, and the root of the chord. HOWEVER, the "ii" chord in a major key is a minor triad. Therefore, the "D" to be covered must be in the "m" column of the bingo card ("m" stands for minor). There is a "D" in the "m" column of the sample card in the Props & Set Design section of this activity. A player using the sample card would be able to cover a space. If there is more than one "D" in that column, only one may be covered.
5. The goal is to cover five spaces in a line across, down, or diagonally. The first player to yell "Bingo" wins the round.
6. Make sure students wait to clear their cards until the spaces of the self-proclaimed winner are verified.
   a. CC - 1 = C in the M column
   b. CC - 2 = D in the m column
   c. CC - 3 = E in the m column
   d. CC - 4 = F in the M column
   e. CC - 5 = G in the M column
   f. CC - 6 = A in the m column
   g. CC - 7 = B in the d column

Encore!!

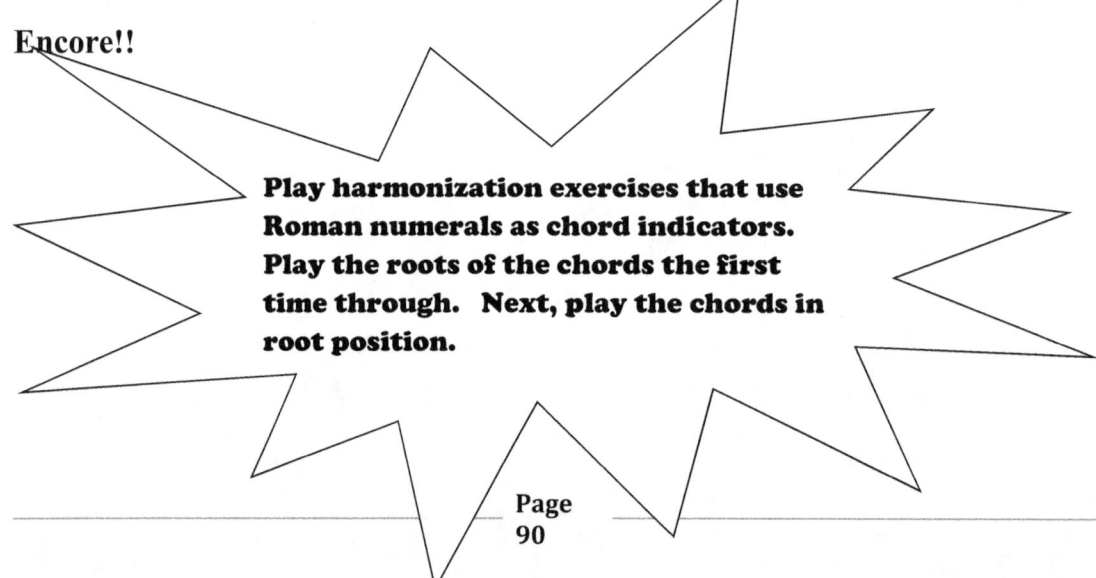

Play harmonization exercises that use Roman numerals as chord indicators. Play the roots of the chords the first time through. Next, play the chords in root position.

Games

Don't Forget!!!

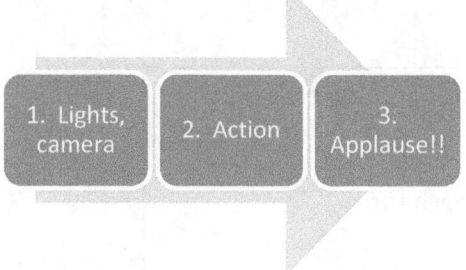

1. Lights, camera
2. Action
3. Applause!!

Important Plot Points

1. <u>Student Action</u> - Start by playing practice rounds while students are learning the rules.

2. <u>Specific Feedback</u> - For the first few rounds, name the letter and column where the chip should be placed. Double check the spaces underneath the winner's winning row to make sure the correct triads were covered. It is wise to place each triad called in a special pile to check answers later.

3. <u>Stunt Work</u> - Point to an example playing card for the correct answer while playing the practice rounds. Also show the triads on a keyboard to help students visualize the triad.

Behind the Scenes

1. **Action-packed.**
Once the rules are clear, avoid big pauses from one triad to the next.

2. **Costuming**

3. **Facial Expressions**
Think Silent Films.

4. **Sound System - Speak clearly.**

5. Rehearsal

Play one or two games, telling the answer after each letter-number combination.

Page 91

The Script:

> The teacher will conduct several complete teaching patterns resembling the following script. They will follow this format:
>
> 1. Teacher calls out the key and scale degree for each turn.
>
> For example:
>
> "F - IV"
>
> 2. Give time for student response.
>
> 3. Teacher Feedback = "You should have covered the B-flat space, under the major (M) column."
>
>
> Teacher presentation: "The letter I call tells you the major scale. The number is the scale degree. If I call "G - ii," you can cover one of the A's in the minor (m) columns. Go ahead and cover it if you have it on your card."
>
> SR
>
> Teacher Feedback: "You are only allowed to cover one space per turn."
>
> Continue in this manner through the practice rounds, until students are confident with the game procedure.

Movement Activities

Movement Activity One

Activity 22: Alberti Calisthenics

Spotlight: Alberti bass

Props & Set Design:
- ✓ Room to move, or a stairwell/staircase
- ✓ Musical pieces or excerpts that have Alberti bass.

Story Board:
1. The goal of this activity is to practice contrasting an Alberti bass and melody (and/or rhythm) by using larger muscle groups.
2. The Alberti bass is played by the feet. The bottom-top-middle-top pattern of the Alberti bass is recreated in the feet by stepping left-right-left-right. The right foot acts as the top note. The left foot alternates between the bottom and middle notes of the pattern. If it is performed on a tile floor, the right foot will always step on the same tile. The left foot will step on the tile that is two tiles to the left of the right foot (This is the bottom note). Then it will step on the tile that is next to the right foot (this is the middle note.).

    Step 1 =   Left (bottom)

Step 2 =   Right (top)
Step 3 =   Left (middle)
Step 4 =   Right (top)

3. Once this is mastered, clap the rhythm of the melody or sing the melody while performing the Alberti bass in the feet.

Re-makes:

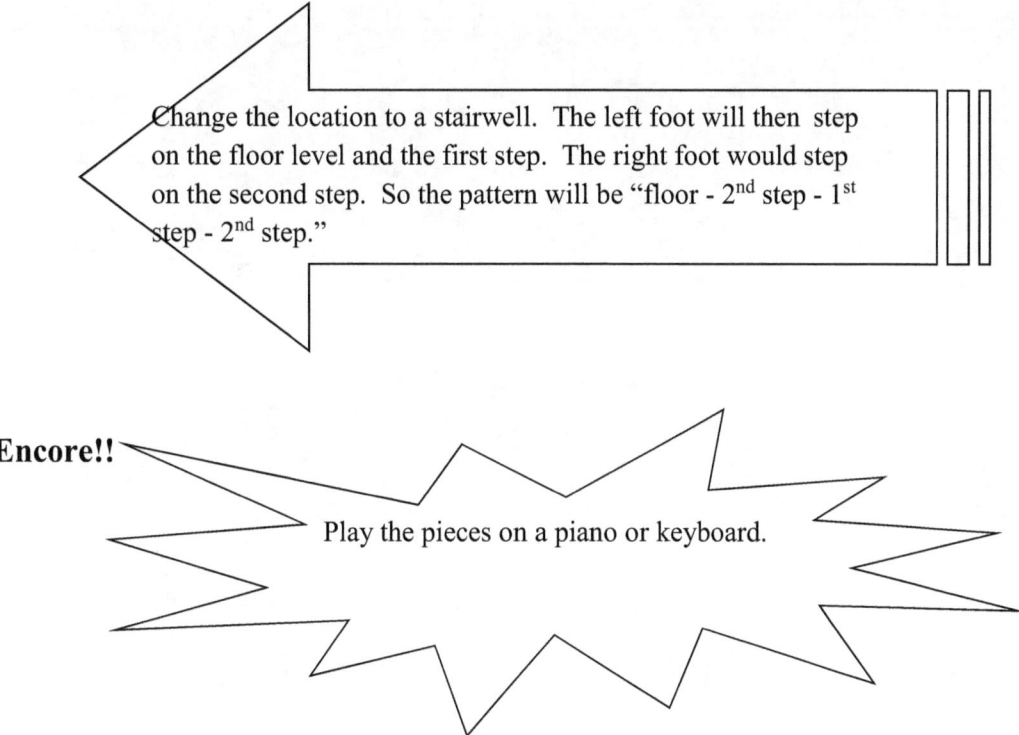

Change the location to a stairwell. The left foot will then step on the floor level and the first step. The right foot would step on the second step. So the pattern will be "floor - 2nd step - 1st step - 2nd step."

Encore!!   Play the pieces on a piano or keyboard.

Don't Forget!!!

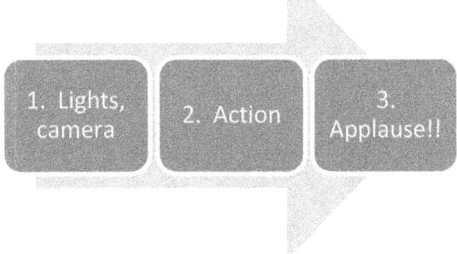

Important Plot Points

1. <u>Student Action</u> - Performing Alberti bass with their feet and clapping or singing the melody.

2. <u>Specific Feedback</u> - Make sure the melody is correctly aligned with the Alberti bass.

3. <u>Stunt Work</u> - Demonstrate the footwork for the Alberti bass.

Behind the Scenes

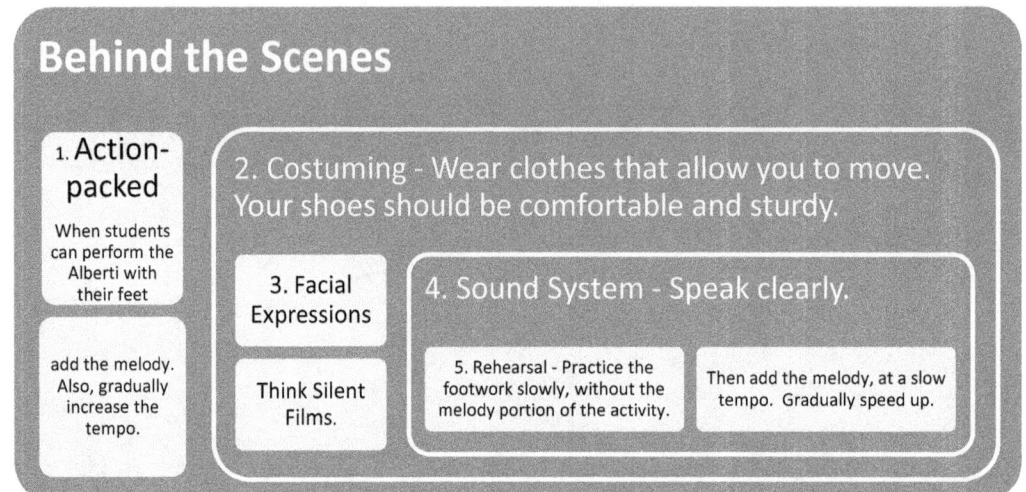

The Script:

> The teacher will conduct several complete teaching patterns resembling the following script. They will follow this format:
>
> 1. Ask students to step, "left-right-left-right."
>
> 2. Give time for student response.
>
> 3. Teacher Feedback = Make sure the left foot is stepping onto the correct tile, or step.
>
>
> Teacher: "Let's start slowly, with our feet only."
>
> Student Response = SR
>
> Teacher Feedback: "Your left foot must alternate between the floor and the first step."

Movement Activity Two

Activity 23: The Shortest Distance Line

Spotlight: Improvisation

Props & Set Design:

- ✓ Room to move. The activity requires a lane for students to walk along. Only one or two students will walk at one time, so the lane will not need to be very wide.

Story Board:

1. The goal of this activity is to encourage students to gain confidence in improvisation at the piano by improvising a way to get from one side of the room to the other.
2. One at a time, students will move from the back of the room to the front of the room. Encourage them to invent a creative way to reach the front of the room. Students may skip, gallop, and turn cartwheels to get to the other side, in addition to other ideas that they might have.
3. After each student has had a chance to go a couple of times, turn on some music that is "dance-able." Ask students to travel down the lane a couple of more times. The music may encourage students to dance across the room.
4. Explain to the students that they were improvising. There was no wrong way to get to the other side of the room. The rule was to get there. Any variation in the task simply makes it more interesting.

Movement Activities

Encore!!

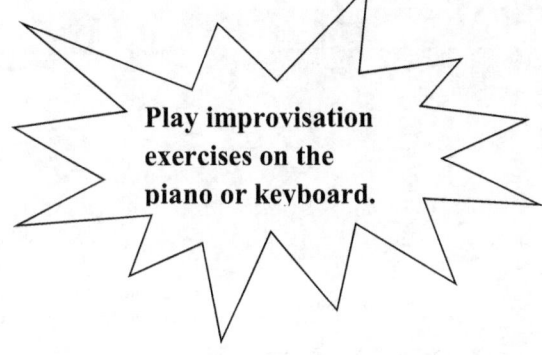

Play improvisation exercises on the piano or keyboard.

Don't Forget!!!

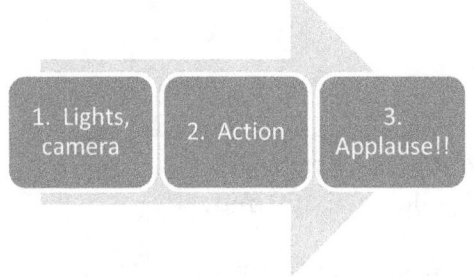

1. Lights, camera
2. Action
3. Applause!!

Important Plot Points

1. <u>Student Action</u> - Improvising ways to cross the room.

2. <u>Specific Feedback</u> - If the students stray from the lane, they should be redirected. Otherwise, there are no incorrect ways to traverse the lane

3. <u>Stunt Work</u> - Demonstrate unique ways to reach the other side of the room.

Movement Activities

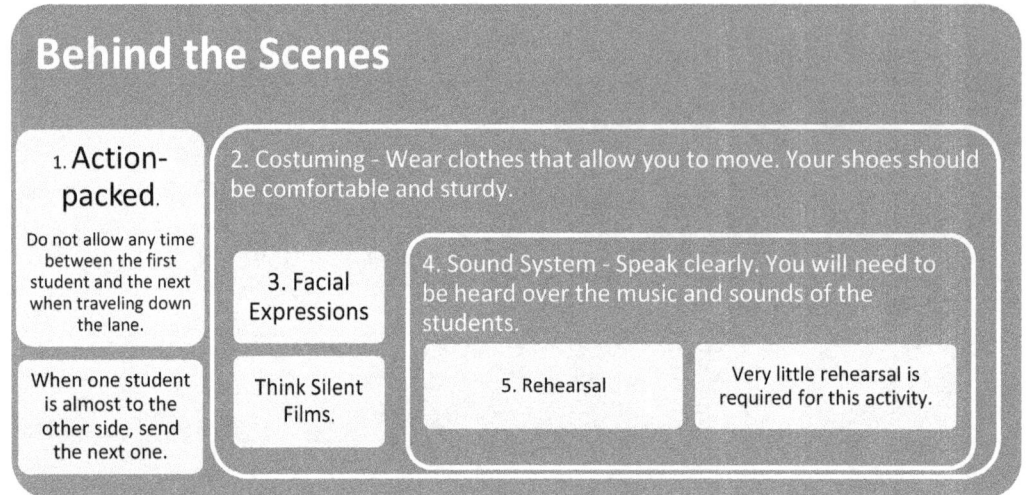

The Script:

The teacher will conduct several complete teaching patterns resembling the following script. They will follow this format:

1. Ask students to travel from one side of the room to the other in a creative manner.

2. Give time for student response.

3. Teacher Feedback =If they are shy at first, tell them to be "silly," "obnoxious," etc.

Teacher: "Your job is to get from this side of the room to the other. Try to do more than walking."

Student Response = SR

Teacher Feedback: "That's a good start. Try strutting or making a weird face."

Movement Activity Three

Activity 24: Grapevine Run

Spotlight: Playing scalar passages at faster tempos.

Props & Set Design:

- ✓ Bath towels, belts, ropes, or sheets.

Story Board:

1. The goal of this activity is to compare the speed of running backwards to the speed of running with a grapevine step.
2. A grapevine step is done by stepping to the right with the right foot. Continue towards the right while crossing the left foot in front of the body and stepping onto the left foot. Then step to the right with the right foot again. Next, continue to the right by crossing the left foot behind the body and stepping onto the left foot. Keep the pattern going. Alternate crossing the left foot in front of, and behind the body. The step may be described as, "step-front-step-behind-step-front-step-behind," and so on.
3. Teach the grapevine step to the students. Ask the students to grapevine across the room as fast as they can. Then ask them to run backwards across the room as fast as they can. Finally ask them to run forward across the room as fast as possible. Hopefully running forwards and backwards will be faster than the grapevine.
4. Then divide the class by assigning partners. One partner will use a rope, belt, towel, or sheet and loop it around the other's mid-section while standing behind him/her. The

Movement Activities

partner (Partner 1) holding the belt, sheet, rope, or towel will pull his partner (Partner 2). Partner 2 will run backwards to feel the difference when s/he is being pulled. It should be easier to run faster when being pulled. The partners will then trade jobs.

5. The partners can do the same thing, running forward. For this portion of the activity the running student will hold onto the rope, belt, sheet, or towel while the pulling partner pulls his/her partner.
6. When students are being pulled, they should feel like their legs do not have to work as hard to move quickly. The same concept should apply to playing scalar passages on the piano.
7. For example:
   When playing an ascending scale with the right hand, turn the right arm so that the fingers are pointing towards the left side of the player's body. Move the elbow out to the side and towards the keyboard so that the right forearm is almost parallel to the fingerboard. Pull your right elbow towards the high end of the keyboard as you play the scale. Your fingers should "crawl" in the direction of you elbow, up the scale.

Encore!!

Practice playing scalar passages in piano pieces using the same concept.

Don't Forget!!!

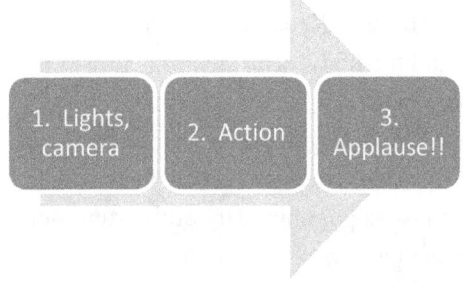

1. Lights, camera
2. Action
3. Applause!!

Page 102

Important Plot Points

1. <u>Student Action</u> - Performing the grapevine and running forwards and backwards across the room.

2. <u>Specific Feedback</u> - Watch the placement of their arms when students are playing scalar passages.

3. <u>Stunt Work</u> - Demonstrate grapevine and playing scalar passages.

Behind the Scenes

1. **Action-packed**.

The grapevine and running portions of the activity should take less than ten minutes.

2. Costuming - Wear shoes that will not fall off when running backwards or doing the grapevine.

3. Facial Expressions

Think Silent Films.

4. Sound System - Speak clearly

5. Rehearsal

Allow students to try the grapevine slowly before they attempt to do it as fast as they can across the room.

The Script:

> The teacher will conduct several complete teaching patterns resembling the following script. They will follow this format:
>
> 1. Ask students to play the scale using the running-versus-grapevine concept.
>
> 2. Give time for student response.
>
> 3. Teacher Feedback =Correct their arm placement if necessary.
>
>
> Teacher: "Try to do the grapevine step as fast as you can to the other side of the room."
>
> Student Response = SR
>
> Teacher Feedback: "Be sure that your left foot alternates stepping in front and back."

Movement Activity Four

Activity 25: Ear-Nose Name Game

Spotlight: Arm/hand independence.

Props & Set Design:

- ✓ No extra materials are necessary.

Story Board:

1. The goal of this game is to do a chant with arm motions to practice arm/hand independence.
2. Students say the following chant while doing the rhythmic coordination exercise explained below.
3. Chant:

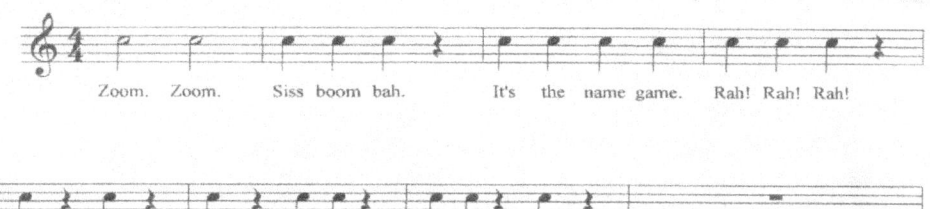

4. Bob starts after the entire group says the first two lines of the chant. He says his own name, then the name of another person in the group (Sue). That person (Sue) repeats her own name then names someone else. The new person, in turn, repeats his/her name then names someone else. This continues until someone breaks the rhythm. A name is said on every beat (when patting the lap).
5. Coordination exercise:
6. Beat 1 = pat the lap with both hands.
7. Beat 2 = simultaneously grab the nose with right hand and grab the right ear with the left hand.
8. Beat 3 = pat the lap with both hands.
9. Beat 4 = simultaneously grab the nose with left hand and grab the left ear with the right hand.
    a. Continue to repeat the coordination, starting with Beat 1.

Encore!!

Play any piece requiring the hands to play independently of each other.

Movement Activities

Don't Forget!!!

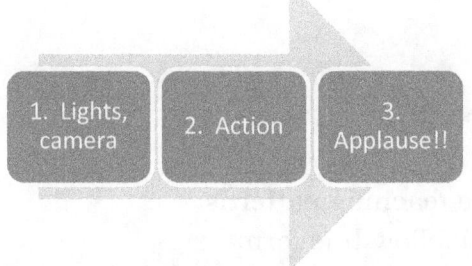

1. Lights, camera
2. Action
3. Applause!!

Important Plot Points

1. <u>Student Action</u> - Performing the coordination exercise.
2. <u>Specific Feedback</u> - Listen carefully to be certain that names are not repeated too often.
3. <u>Stunt Work</u> - Demonstrate the motion of the hands and arms.

Behind the Scenes

1. **Action-packed.** As soon the students feel comfortable with the coordination exercise, begin the game.
2. Costuming - Wear a shirt that allows full movement of the arms.
3. Facial Expressions - Think Silent Films.
4. Sound System - Speak clearly teacher and students should say the chant and names with confidence.
5. Rehearsal - Begin the coordination exercise very slowly. Gradually speed up to a Moderato tempo.

The Script:

> The teacher will conduct several complete teaching patterns resembling the following script. They will follow this format:
>
> 1. Say the first phrase of the chant. Tell students to repeat what you said, in rhythm.
>
> 2. Give time for student response.
>
> 3. Teacher Feedback = Correct incorrectly spoken rhythms.
>
> Teacher: "After you tap your lap, try to grab your nose with your right and grab your right ear with your left hand like this. You have to grab your ear and your nose at the same time, like this."
>
> Student Response = SR
>
> Teacher Feedback: "Don't wait to grab your ear until after you've found your nose. Try to grab them at the same time."
>
> Start slowly and gradually accelerando.

Movement Activity Five

Activity 26: Brain/Arm Teaser

Spotlight: Reading two things, and performing two tasks at the same time.

Props & Set Design:

- ✓ Posterboard with the letters of the alphabet and symbols indicating various body percussion tasks.
- ✓ Example of the poster:

A	B	C	D	E	p = pat your knees
p	c	s	c	p	c = clap your hands
F	G	H	I	J	s = snap your fingers
s	p	c	s	s	
K	L	M	N	O	
c	s	p	p	c	
P	Q	R	S	T	
c	c	s	p	s	
U	V	W	X	Y	Z
c	p	s	p	c	p

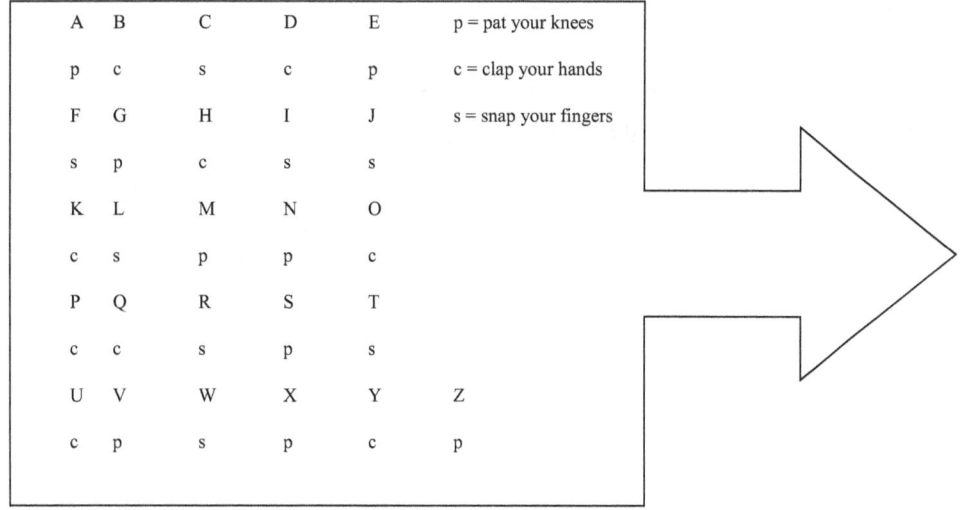

Story Board:

1. The goal of this activity is to say the letter of the alphabet while performing the body percussion task. For the example above, the students will say "A," while patting their knees. Then they will say "B" while clapping their hands ... "C" while snapping the fingers, etc.
2. The challenge of this activity is that the students must read both the letter of the alphabet and the body percussion symbol, simultaneously. They must also perform two actions (stating the letter and performing the task), simultaneously. In order to succeed at this activity, a student will need to look ahead to see which action is coming up. The same skill is required when sightreading a piece of music.

Re-makes:

Rearrange the order of body percussion tasks, or add more task possibilities.

Encore!!

Sightread pieces of music at the appropriate level for your students.

Don't Forget!!!

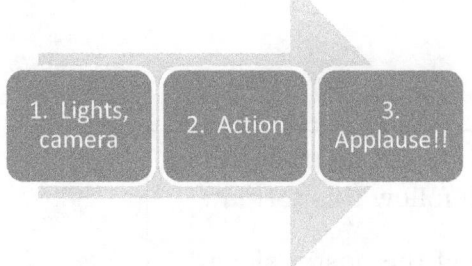

1. Lights, camera
2. Action
3. Applause!!

Important Plot Points

1. <u>Student Action</u> - Saying the letter names and performing the body percussion tasks.

2. <u>Specific Feedback</u> - Correcting incorrect letters, or body percussion. Reminding students to look ahead.

3. <u>Stunt Work</u> - Demonstrating the activity

Behind the Scenes

1. **Action-packed.** Have multiple poster prepared so that students have new combinations to try out.

2. Costuming - Wear shoes that will not fall off when running backwards or doing the grapevine.

3. Facial Expressions. Think Silent Films.

4. Sound System - Say the letters loudly and clearly.

5. Rehearsal. Begin slowly, with the first line.

The Script:

> The teacher will conduct several complete teaching patterns resembling the following script. They will follow this format:
>
> 1. Ask students to perform the first line of the poster slowly.
>
> 2. Give time for student response.
>
> 3. Teacher Feedback = Remind students to look ahead to see what is coming up.
>
> Teacher: "Let's perform the second line."
>
> Student Response = SR
>
> Teacher Feedback: "Try not to pause between letters. If you look ahead, you won't need to stop in the middle."

Credits:

> The idea for this activity was inspired by *Ready-to-use motor skills & movement station lesson plans for young children,* written by Landy & Burridge (2000).

Group Work

Group Work One

Activity 27: The Apprentice

Spotlight: Practicing, analyzing, and performing ensembles

Props & Set Design:
- ✓ At least two different keyboard ensemble pieces.
- ✓ Enough parts and/or copies for every student in each ensemble.

Story Board:
1. The goal of this activity is for students to perform ensemble pieces as well as possible. This includes musicality and playing as an ensemble, in addition to playing the right notes.
2. The activity is patterned after the television show of the same name. Divide the class into two teams or ensembles. Have each ensemble select a project manager. It is that person's job to oversee the rehearsal and preparation of the piece, as well as perform in the ensemble. Allow each group plenty of practice time to prepare their pieces. At the end of the preparation time, each group is to perform.
3. Bring in outside judges to determine which group is the winning group. These may be faculty members, or students from another class. Have them decide by secret scoring cards to avoid any hurt feelings. The winning group progresses to the next round. That group is divided into two smaller ensembles. Each group selects a new project manager. Allow them practice time to prepare their pieces. Let them perform them. The winning

ensemble progresses to the next round. Divide the winning group into two smaller groups. Continue the process in the same manner until the final four, or three. If there are four remaining, the competition will be between two duets. The members of the winning duet are the new apprentices. If there are three remaining, there will be three apprentices.

Re-makes:

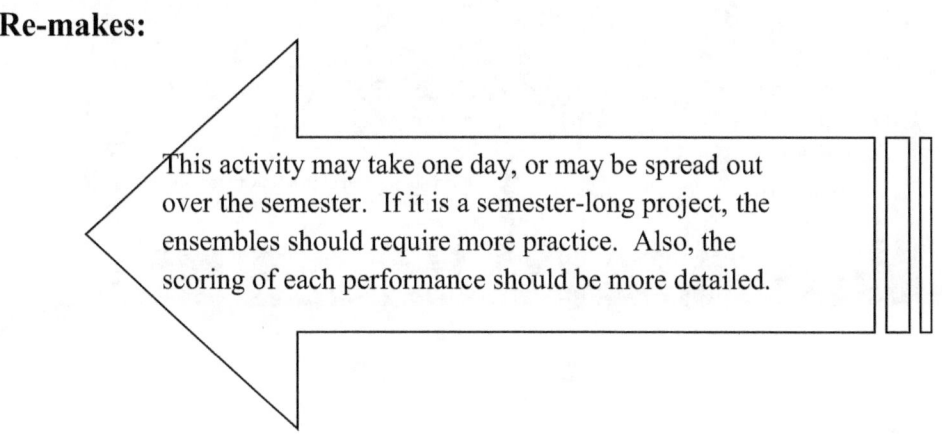

This activity may take one day, or may be spread out over the semester. If it is a semester-long project, the ensembles should require more practice. Also, the scoring of each performance should be more detailed.

Don't Forget!!!

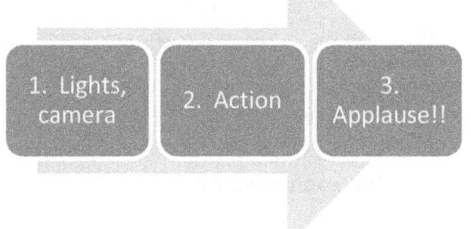

1. Lights, camera
2. Action
3. Applause!!

Important Plot Points

1. <u>Student Action</u> - Rehearsing and collaborating on the ensembles.

2. <u>Specific Feedback</u> - Specific feedback will come from the project manager and other group members.

3. <u>Stunt Work</u> - Alternate placing yourself near each group to assist them if necessary. This also reminds them to tend to the task.

Group Work

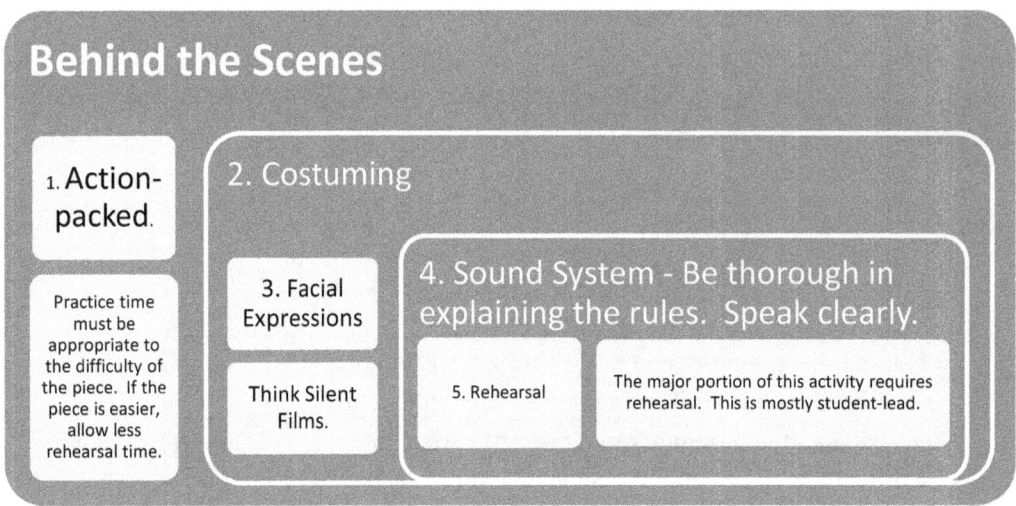

The Script:

The teacher will conduct several complete teaching patterns resembling the following script. They will follow this format:

1. Ask students to practice the ensembles and perform them.

2. Give time for student response.

3. Teacher Feedback = Point out certain musical aspects that each ensemble successfully included in their performances.

Teacher: "Ok. It is time to perform our pieces. Let's start with Group 1."

Student Response = SR

Teacher Feedback: "I can tell that Group 1 focused on dynamic contrasts."

Group Work Two

Activity 28: Animated Feature

Spotlight: Creating feeling or meaning for piano repertoire.

Props & Set Design:
- ✓ Piano repertoire pieces. Romantic, programmatic, or contemporary pieces are the most appropriate for this activity. However, other styles will work as well.

Story Board:

The goal of this activity is to encourage students to view piano pieces as abstract messages to an audience rather than mere notes on a page.

1. Divide the class into groups. Assign a different short repertoire piece or section of a longer repertoire piece to each group. Each group is to create a story that the members will pantomime to the music assigned to them. Once every group has practiced their stories, the stories will be performed for the rest of the class.

Re-makes:

Instead of writing stories, the groups could choreograph a dance or interpretive movement for their assigned music.

Encore!!

Play the pieces with the stories in mind.

Don't Forget!!!

1. Lights, camera
2. Action
3. Applause!!

Important Plot Points

| 1. Student Action - Pantomiming the stories along with the music. | 2. Specific Feedback - Emphasize the idea that the animation should fit the music. | 3. Stunt Work - Demonstrate possible storylines to go with small sections of music. |

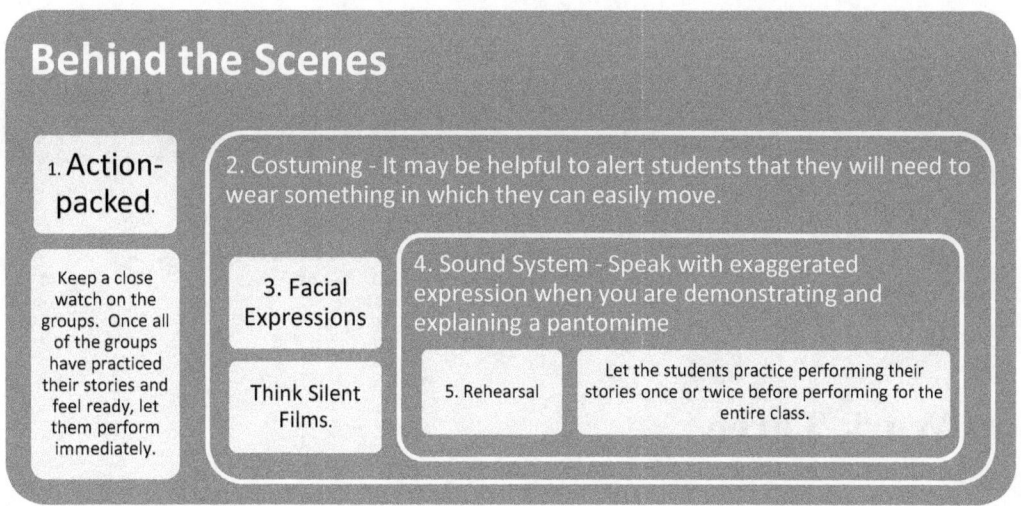

The Script:

> The teacher will conduct several complete teaching patterns resembling the following script. They will follow this format:
>
> 1. Ask students to create a story to go with the music, then act it out.
>
> 2. Give time for student response.
>
> 3. Teacher Feedback = Remind students that bigger facial expressions and gestures will help the audience understand what is happening in the story.
>
> Teacher: "Write a story to go with the B section of this piece."
>
> Student Response = SR
>
> Teacher Feedback: "Be sure to synchronize the story with the music as well as you can."

Group Work Three

Activity 29: Make a Scene

Spotlight: Theme and Variations

Props & Set Design:

- ✓ This activity may require a wide range of props, depending on what the teacher selects for the scene. If you follow the exact recommendation given in this activity, you will need at least one table for each group.
- ✓ The provision of additional props is left to the teacher's discretion.

Story Board:

1. The goal of this activity is to explain theme and variation form by creating a scene.
2. Divide the class into two or three groups. Ask each group to create a visual scene (they may add audio if they prefer.), given only vague descriptions.

For Example:

Each group is supposed to create a scene with three people at a table, at a party. Do not provide any further descriptions. This allows students to make the party a dinner party, birthday party, New Year's Eve party, etc. They may have people eating, drinking tea, arguing, playing poker, etc. There may, or may not be people in the background. Some scenes may have background music, or people talking. Some groups may choose to narrate their scenes. There are many possible variations.

The theme is "Three people, at a table, at a party." Though there are several variations, the theme should still be detectable in each scene.

Re-makes:

You may select a different "theme." Just be sure to be vague.

Encore!!

Explain the relationship between the activity and piano pieces that are theme and variations. Each variation to the theme may seem quite different, but the basic elements of the theme are still present.

Don't Forget!!!

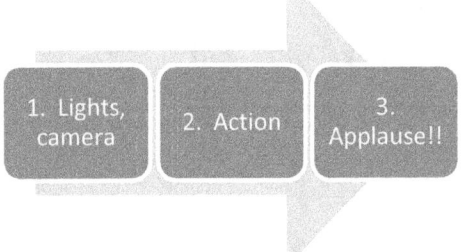

Important Plot Points

| 1. <u>Student Action</u> - Creating and posing in a scene. | 2. <u>Specific Feedback</u> - Insist that the basic elements of the theme are included in each scene. | 3. <u>Stunt Work</u> - Posing and/or demonstrating different possibilities for a scene. |

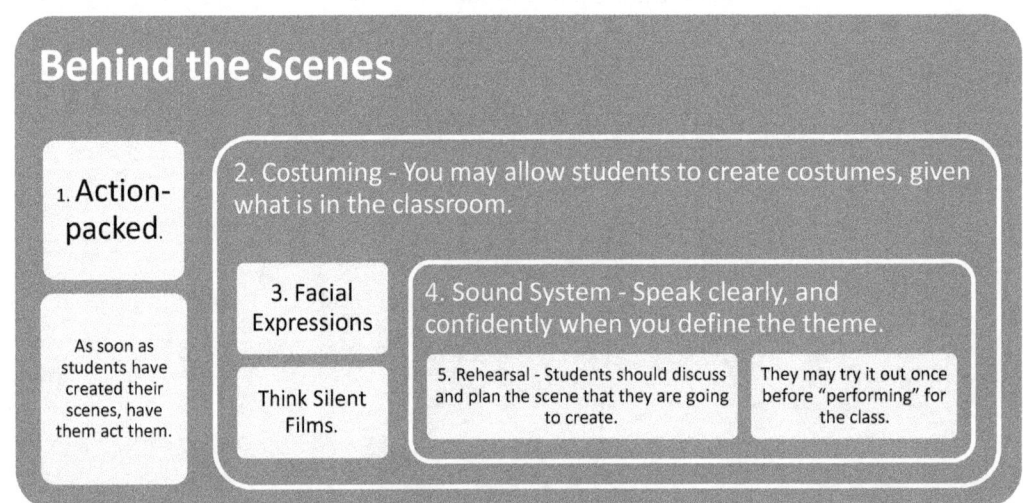

The Script:

> The teacher will conduct several complete teaching patterns resembling the following script. They will follow this format:
>
> 1. Ask students to create a scene that has three people at a table, at a party.
>
> 2. Give time for student response.
>
> 3. Teacher Feedback =Check each scene to make sure they fit the criteria described in the theme (for example: Three people – No more. No less.)
>
>
> Teacher: "Now Group One should create their scene."
>
> Student Response = SR
>
> Teacher Feedback: "This scene is good because there are exactly three people. They are at a table and at a party too."

Group Work Four

Activity 30: Electric Statues

Spotlight: Encouraging musicality.

Props & Set Design:

- ✓ Some space for students to move.

Story Board:

1. The goal of this activity is to encourage students to play musically by making poses that have energy.
2. Each student should select or be assigned to a partner. One person is the "clay" that will be molded into a statue. The other person is the "artist." The "artist" moves the "clay's" arms, hands, legs, and feet into a pose to make the "clay" into a statue. The statue must imagine that there is a big light switch. The "artist" should then flip the switch. Once the switch is flipped, the statue must imagine that electricity is radiating towards his/her fingertips and toes. However, no audible traces of electricity should be heard (Statues must resist the urge to "buzz.").
3. If the statue begins to vibrate, ask the artist to turn the switch off. Then tell the statue to try not to vibrate the next time the switch is flipped, even though electricity is still radiating to the fingertips and toes.
4. The desired result is that the statue's muscles will tighten somewhat.

Encore!!

Play piano exercises and/or pieces while sending electricity or energy into

Don't Forget!!!

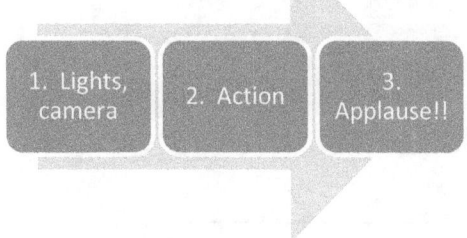

Important Plot Points

1. <u>Student Action</u> - Molding statues and posing as statues. Flipping the light switch and radiating electricity.	2. <u>Specific Feedback</u> - Remind statues not to "buzz" or vibrate when the electricity is flowing.	3. <u>Stunt Work</u> - Demonstrate an electric statue.

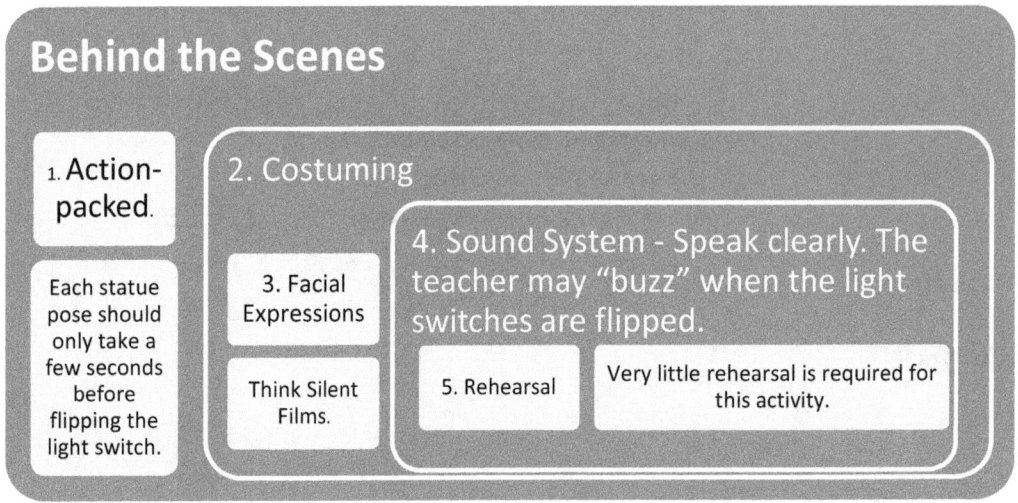

The Script:

> The teacher will conduct several complete teaching patterns resembling the following script. They will follow this format:
>
> 1. Ask students to have one partner move the other partners arms and legs into a pose for a statue.
>
> 2. Give time for student response.
>
> 3. Teacher Feedback =The more dramatic the pose, the better.
>
> Teacher: "'Artist,' please flip the light switch so the statue has electricity."
>
> Student Response = SR
>
> Teacher Feedback: "Statue, try not to vibrate as a result of the electricity."

Group Work Five

Activity 31: Baroque Imitation

Spotlight: Imitation in Baroque music.

Props & Set Design:

✓ No extra materials are required.

Story Board:

1. The goal of this activity is to emphasize the idea that Baroque music often has more than one voice that carries a melodic line. In imitation, one voice starts, then another begins using the same melody later in the piece. However, the melody may change slightly towards the end of the phrase.
2. Some students will read a script that does verbally what a Bach Invention does musically.

An Example Script:

Voice 1: "I really love to watch the movies, especially when I can get popcorn, candy and soda." (Continue reading Voice 1, even when Voice 2 begins reading.). "My favorite kind of movie is action-adventure. The ones with car chases and action sequences are the most exciting. However, I like action sequences a little bit more."

Voice 2: (Wait until Voice 1 finishes saying the word, "movies," then begin reading your line.) "I really love to watch the movies, especially when I can get popcorn, and soda. My favorite genre is action-adventure. The most exciting scenes are action sequences. Car chases come in a close second."

Voice 2: "Movies that have passionate musical scores to go with them are even more interesting. Something about the music helps the audience connect emotionally with what is happening on the screen. Sometimes the music swells during the sad parts of the movies. It makes some people cry, but not me. I am too interested in the relationship the music has with the events in the movies. (Say the next part slowly, with Voice 1). I ... love ... movies."

Voice 1: (Wait until Voice 2 finishes saying the word, "musical," then begin reading your line). "Movies that have passionate musical scores are interesting. (Read the next part slowly.) The music helps the audience connect emotionally. The music swells when it is sad and makes people cry. (Wait until Voice 2 finishes saying, "the relationship the music has with the events in the movies," then say the next part slowly, with Voice 2). I ... love ... movies."

Re-makes:

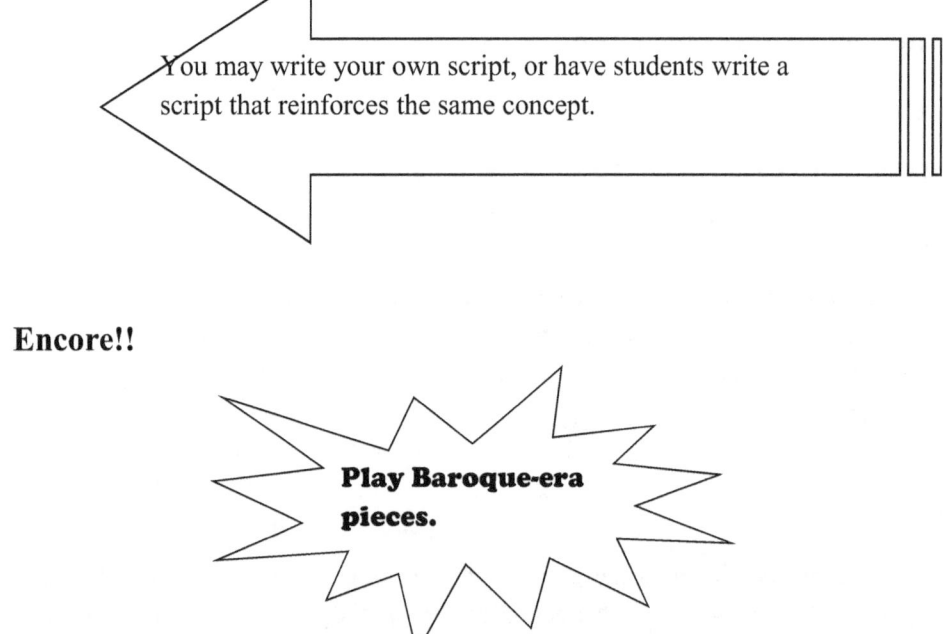

You may write your own script, or have students write a script that reinforces the same concept.

Encore!!

Play Baroque-era pieces.

Don't Forget!!!

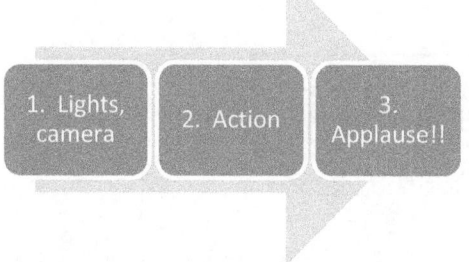

Important Plot Points

1. <u>Student Action</u> - Have students move with the flash cards as you explain the object of the game. Vary the tempos and how far ahead the students must look.

2. <u>Specific Feedback</u> - Correcting the dance step. Remind them to look ahead, and not at their feet. Make sure to let everyone know the correct step after each attempt.

3. <u>Stunt Work</u> - You will need to demonstrate the dance steps until the students understand how the game is played.

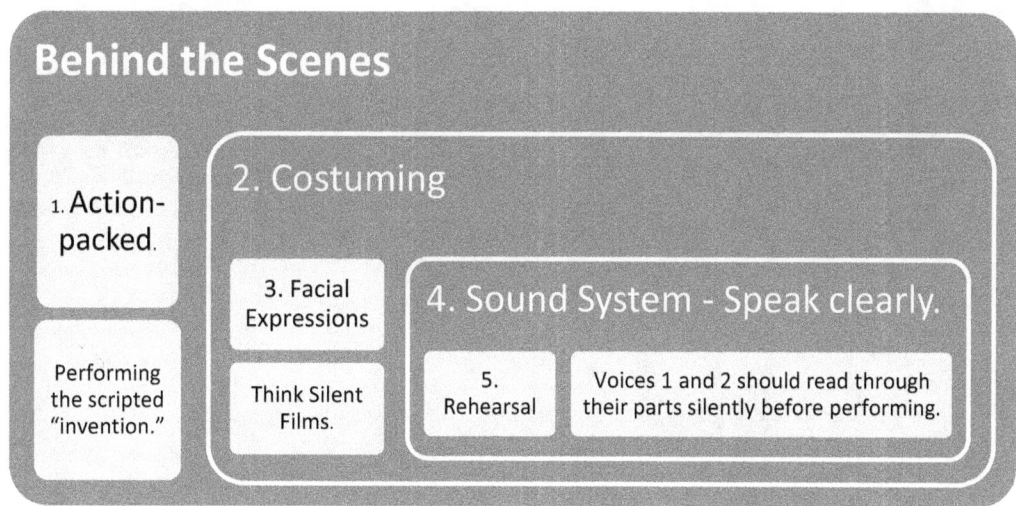

The Script:

> The teacher will conduct several complete teaching patterns resembling the following script. They will follow this format:
>
> 1. Ask students to read the script aloud for the class.
>
> 2. Give time for student response.
>
> 3. Teacher Feedback =Make sure you pause when the script asks for it, and say unison parts together.
>
>
> Teacher: "Read the script aloud to the class."
>
> Student Response = SR
>
> Teacher Feedback: "Read your part with feeling. One part is not necessarily more important than the other."

Group Work Six

Activity 32: Recreate this Photo

Spotlight: Different stylistic eras of piano literature history.

Different forms in piano literature.

Props & Set Design:

- ✓ Giant picture frames. These can be created out of paper or wood. The height should be close to the height of the ceiling. The width may vary, depending on the room size or the space available within the room.
- ✓ Other props can be random. Students will pick and choose from the selection to help create their photos. It is best to provide a wide range of props (interesting hats, stuffed animals, baseball bats, bicycle wheels, blankets, kitchen utensils, holiday decorations, and other unique objects.).

Story Board:

1. The goal of this activity is to make students identify elements of certain musical styles or forms and then transfer those elements to an imaginary photograph.
2. Divide the class into groups of six to ten. Assign a musical form or style to each group. Students must then make a list of characteristics of that form or style. They should try to come up with as many characteristics as they can.
3. Once all groups have had sufficient time to make their lists, they must create a photo that has the elements that are on the list. The photo does not have to have a musical theme.

Encourage students to be creative. The photo should be "life-sized." Members of each group may pose as people in the photo.

4. Groups take turns "displaying" their photos. One member of each group should be designated to explain the elements of the photo and how it represents the musical style or form for that group.

Re-makes:

It is not absolutely necessary to use the giant picture frames. They just help create the entire "photo" concept.

Encore!!

Play pieces from the musical styles or forms

Group Work

Don't Forget!!!

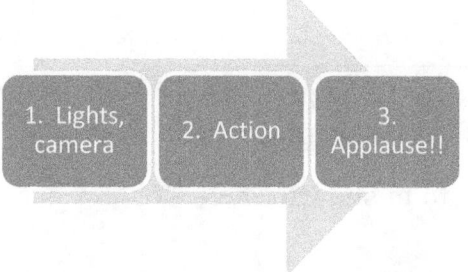

Important Plot Points

1. <u>Student Action</u> - Listing elements of musical styles and forms. Creating and posing for life-sized photos.

2. <u>Specific Feedback</u> - the teacher may want to check the list of characteristics before students create the photo.

3. <u>Stunt Work</u> - Demonstrate and explain possible ways to put characteristics of the musical styles and forms into a photo.

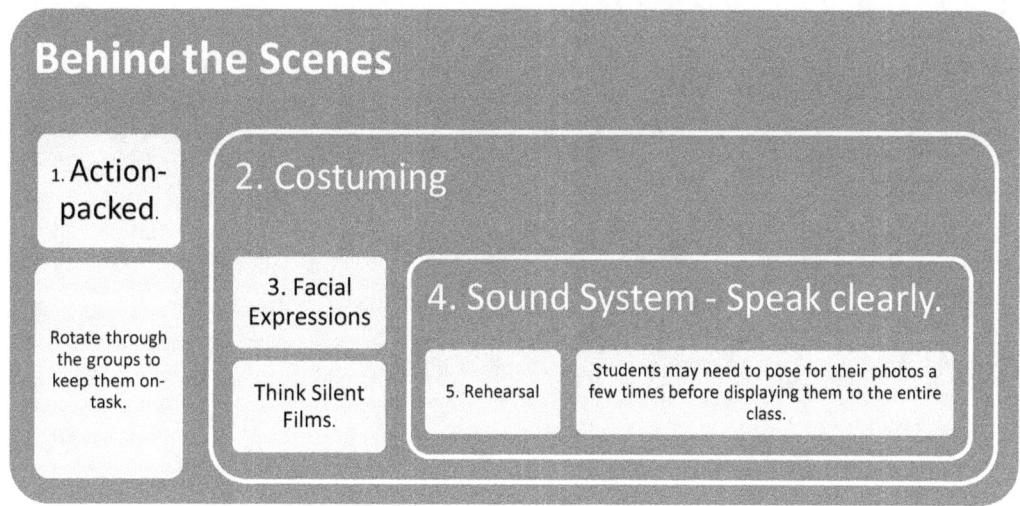

Page 133

The Script:

> The teacher will conduct several complete teaching patterns resembling the following script. They will follow this format:
>
> 1. Ask students to create a life-sized photo to show to the class.
>
> 2. Give time for student response.
>
> 3. Teacher Feedback =If certain characteristics or elements are left out, mention those elements after groups have explained their photos.
>
>
> Teacher: "What elements do you have listed for sonata form?"
>
> Student Response = SR
>
> Teacher Feedback: "You can include the Tonic-Dominant relationship too."

Group Work Seven

Activity 33: Classical Voices

Spotlight: Balancing right-hand melody with a left-hand chordal accompaniment in Classic-era music.

Props & Set Design:

- ✓ No extra materials are required.

Story Board:

1. The goal of this activity is to demonstrate that the melody in the right hand is supported by the left hand in Classic-era keyboard music.
2. Some students will read a script that does verbally what Classic-era keyboard pieces do musically.

Example Script:

Voice 1: "I really love to watch the movies, especially when I can get popcorn, candy and soda." (Continue reading Voice 1, even when Voice 2 begins reading.).

Voice 2: "So do I!"

Voice 1: "My favorite kind of movie is action-adventure. The ones with car chases and action sequences are the most exciting. However, I like action sequences a little bit more."

Voice 2: "Fight scenes are great!"

Voice 1: "Movies that have passionate musical scores to go with them are even more interesting."

Voice 2: "That's true."

Voice 1: "Something about the music helps the audience connect emotionally with what is happening on the screen."

Voice 2: "Beautiful."

Voice 1: "Sometimes the music swells during the sad parts of the movies. It makes some people cry, but not me."

Voice 2: "Crying is for babies."

Voice1: "I am too interested in the relationship the music has with the events in the movies. (Say the next part slowly, with Voice 2). I ... love ... movies."

Voice 2: (Say this part slowly, with Voice 1) "I ... love ... movies."

Re-makes:

You may write your own script, or have students write a script that reinforces the same concept.

Encore!!

Play Classic-era pieces.

Group Work

Don't Forget!!!

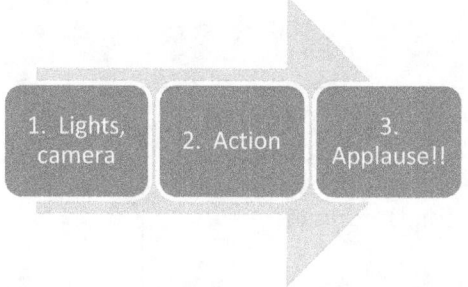

1. Lights, camera
2. Action
3. Applause!!

Important Plot Points

1. <u>Student Action</u> - Performing the Classic-era script.

2. <u>Specific Feedback</u> - Make sure Voices 1 and 2 perform the script exactly as it is written (even with the pacing notes.).

3. <u>Stunt Work</u> - Demonstrate a portion of the script.

Behind the Scenes

1. **Action-packed.** Give the performers a chance to read through their parts, the have them perform right away.

2. **Costuming**

3. **Facial Expressions** Think Silent Films.

4. **Sound System - Speak clearly.**

5. **Rehearsal** Voices 1 and 2 should read through their parts silently before performing.

The Script:

> The teacher will conduct several complete teaching patterns resembling the following script. They will follow this format:
>
> 1. Ask students to read the script aloud for the class.
>
> 2. Give time for student response.
>
> 3. Teacher Feedback =Make sure you pause when the script asks you to, and say unison parts together.
>
>
> Teacher: "Read the script aloud to the class."
>
> Student Response = SR
>
> Teacher Feedback: "Voice 2 is the left hand, and should be in support of Voice 1 (the right hand)."

Group Work Eight

Activity 34: The Brown Suit

Spotlight: Theme and Variations

Props & Set Design:
- ✓ Pieces of paper, colored pencils, crayons, markers, scissors, glue, glitter, etc.

Story Board:
1. The goal of this activity is to explain theme and variation form by designing a brown suit.
2. Ask each student to design a "brown suit." The teacher will also design one. Each student is to draw his/her design on a piece of paper. Any art materials may be used to add to make the suit more (or less) aesthetically pleasing. Do not specify anything else about the suit, other than the fact that it is brown. This leaves students several with options for their designs. Students may create suits for either men or women. It is even possible that someone will design a swimsuit.
3. The teacher's "brown suit" will be only a brown suit. It will be a brown jacket, brown pair of pants, and a shirt. The suit will be a man's suit. Do not add any embellishments to the suit.
4. The teacher will display his/her suit first. This will be the theme.
5. Then the students will show their suits. These are the variations. Though there are several variations, the theme should still be detectable in each suit.

Re-makes:

⬅ You may select a different "theme." Just be sure to be vague.

Encore!!

Explain the relationship between the activity and piano pieces that are theme and variations. Each variation to the theme may seem quite different, but the basic elements of the theme are still present.

Don't Forget!!!

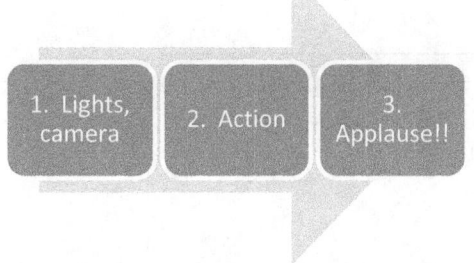

Important Plot Points

1. <u>Student Action</u> - Designing and decorating "brown suits."

2. <u>Specific Feedback</u> - Insist that the basic elements of the theme are included in each suit.

3. <u>Stunt Work</u> - Show your "brown suit," but not until after students are done designing theirs.

Behind the Scenes

1. **Action-packed.** As soon as students are done designing their suits, have them show them.

2. Costuming

3. Facial Expressions. Think Silent Films.

4. Sound System - Speak clearly and confidently when you define the theme.

5. Rehearsal. It may be wise to draw the suit in pencil before adding embellishments and details.

The Script:

> The teacher will conduct several complete teaching patterns resembling the following script. They will follow this format:
>
> 1. Ask students to design a "brown suit."
>
> 2. Give time for student response.
>
> 3. Teacher Feedback =Check each suit to make sure they fit the criteria described in the theme. Each one must be some type of suit, and it must be brown.
>
>
> Teacher: "Row 2, show us your suits."
>
> Student Response = SR
>
> Teacher Feedback: "This suit is good, even though it is for a woman and has a skirt. It is brown, which stays true to the theme. The hat is a nice variation too."

Group Work Nine

Activity 35: Build a House

Spotlight: Practicing a repertoire piece.

Props & Set Design:
- ✓ Shoe boxes, glue, scissors, construction paper, markers, crayons, glitter, dollhouse furniture, etc.

Story Board:
1. The goal of this activity is to build a diorama of a room in a house, complete with decorations. The steps to designing and decorating the room serve as an analogy to rehearsing a repertoire piece for performance.
2. Ask students to use the decorations and art supplies provided to create a diorama of a room in a house.
3. Explain the similarities to preparing piano repertoire:
    a. Step 1: Make sure all of the basic elements are in place (For the room – furniture; for the piano – notes and rhythm).
    b. Step 2: Add aesthetic elements (For the room – decorations; for the piano – dynamics, articulation, tempo, etc.).
    c. Step 3: Clean up (For the room – dusting and polishing; for the piano – clean up difficult passages.).

d. Step 4: Add the personal touch. (For the room – family photos, etc.; for the piano – personal interpretation including additional rubatos, distinct phrasing, etc.).

Encore!!

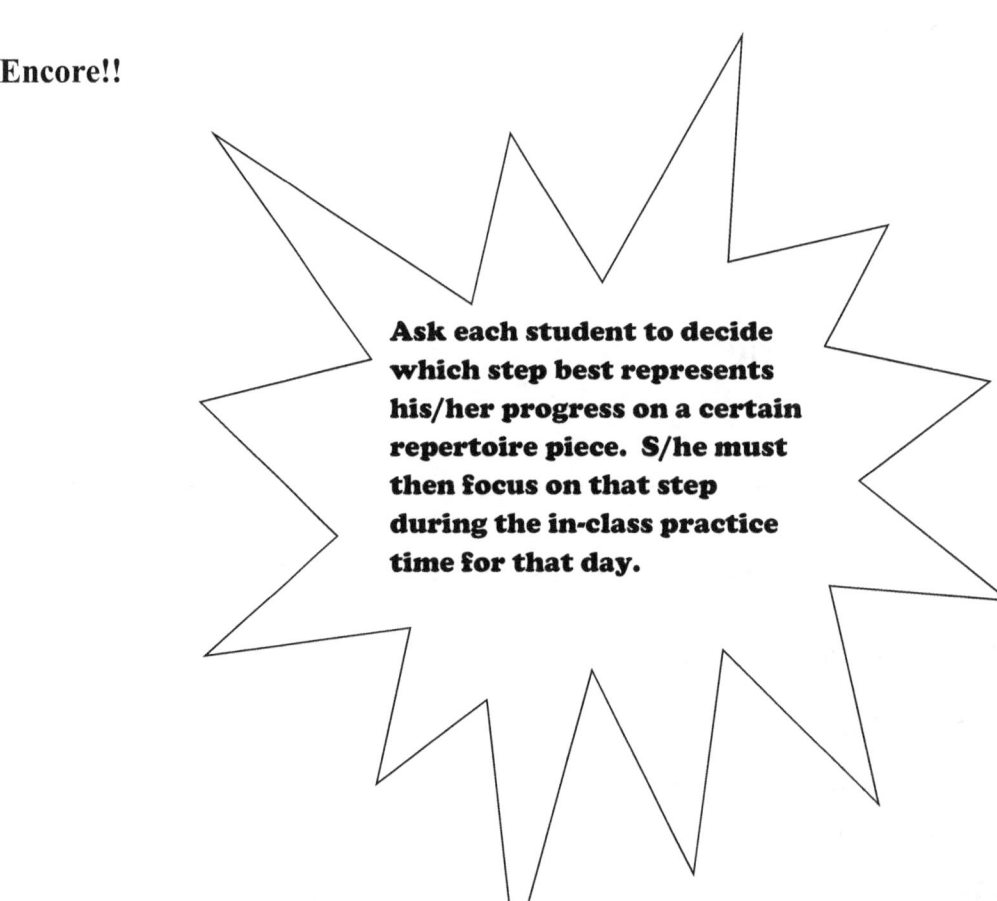

Ask each student to decide which step best represents his/her progress on a certain repertoire piece. S/he must then focus on that step during the in-class practice time for that day.

Don't Forget!!!

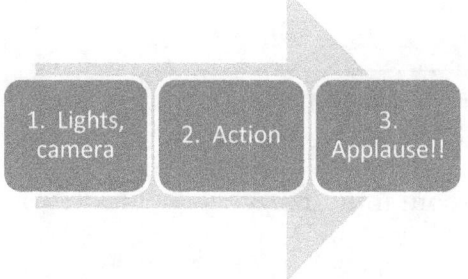

Important Plot Points

1. <u>Student Action</u> - Designing and decorating dioramas.

2. <u>Specific Feedback</u> - Ask students to pay attention to detail when building their dioramas.

3. <u>Stunt Work</u> Show students how certain parts of the diorama might be created.

Behind the Scenes

1. **Action-packed**. If some students finish faster than others, you may have the steps listed on a piece of paper with directions on what to practice.

Hand out copies of the paper as each student finishes.

2. Costuming

3. Facial Expressions

Think Silent Films.

4. Sound System - Speak clearly.

5. Rehearsal

Students might be more detailed if the diorama is a take-home activity.

The Script:

> The teacher will conduct several complete teaching patterns resembling the following script. They will follow this format:
>
> 1. Ask students to build a diorama of a room in a home.
>
> 2. Give time for student response.
>
> 3. Teacher Feedback =Ask them to add details to distinguish each room from the others in the class.
>
>
> Teacher: "Now that you have the basics for the room, go ahead and add decorations."
>
> Student Response = SR
>
> Teacher Feedback: "The cleaner looking the room, the more inviting it will seem."

Group Work Ten

Activity 36: Guests at a Party

Spotlight: Playing as expressively as possible.

Props & Set Design:

- ✓ Room for students to perform a skit.

Story Board:

1. The goal of this activity is to make students use verbal clues and acting skills to help one student figure out the distinct characters at an imaginary party.
2. One student portrays the host of a party. The host must interact with the guests to help discover what each guest is.
3. For example:
    a. Guests can be a

    "Movie star who is trying to escape the paparazzi."

    "Little boy looking for his lost dog."

    "Octopus."

    "Mechanic who thinks he's a super hero."

    "Presidential candidate."

"Retired Rockette."

"Broadway choreographer."

"Sound-effects guy."

"Obsessive marathon runner."

"Drunk meteorologist."

4. One at a time, guests arrive and have conversations or encounters with their host. Each guest should act like his/her character. The only rule is that the guests may not use key words that describe their characters.
    a. For example:

    "Little boy looking for his lost dog" may not ask, "Have you seen my dog?"

    "Mechanic who thinks he's a super hero" may not announce, "I'm Batman!"

5. As the host identifies each guest, that guest will leave the party. The activity ends when every guest is correctly identified.
6. It will be difficult for both the guests and the host if the guests' clues are understated. They will need to exaggerated the idiosyncracies of their characters.

Re-makes:

Allow students to make up their own characters. The more obscure and specific, the better. A generalized character (Like dancer, dog, singer, skier, cat, cow, etc.) will be too easy to act out and/or identify.

Encore!!

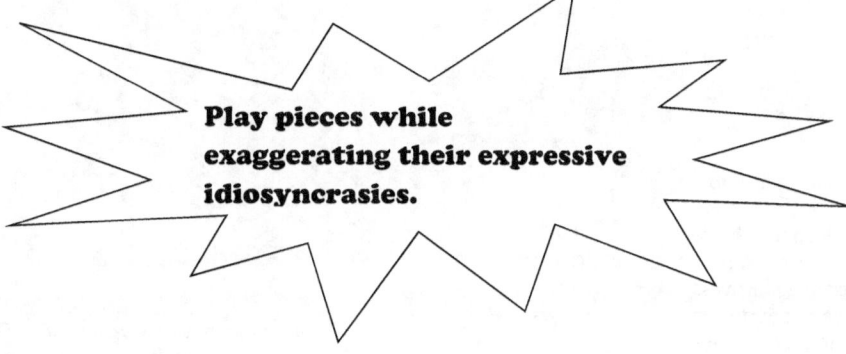

Play pieces while exaggerating their expressive idiosyncrasies.

Don't Forget!!!

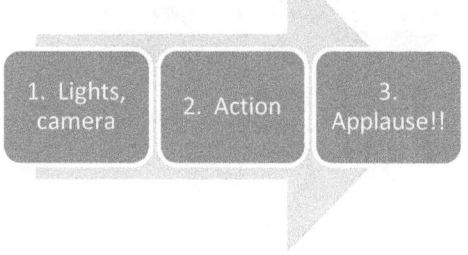

1. Lights, camera
2. Action
3. Applause!!

Important Plot Points

| 1. <u>Student Action</u> - Acting like their assigned characters. | 2. <u>Specific Feedback</u> - Do not let students use obvious announcements of who s/he is unless the host is struggling to identify him/her. | 3. <u>Stunt Work</u> - Show how one might act like a specific guest. |

Behind the Scenes

1. Action-packed

Give each guest about 30 seconds to introduce him/herself to the host before the next guest arrives. Once the party has progressed a while, allow the guests to be more obvious with their clues.

2. Costuming

3. Facial Expressions

Think Silent Films.

4. Sound System - Use accents if they pertain to the characters of the guests.

5. Rehearsal

Guests can have a few seconds to think about how they will present themselves before arriving at the party.

The Script:

> The teacher will conduct several complete teaching patterns resembling the following script. They will follow this format:
>
> 1. Ask students to act out the descriptions of their characters.
>
> 2. Give time for student response.
>
> 3. Teacher Feedback =Do not let them use significant words that were used in the descriptions of their characters.
>
>
> Teacher: "The next guest has arrived."
>
> Student Response = SR
>
> Teacher Feedback: "'Presidential candidate' - you weren't supposed to say that you were running for president. That makes it too easy."

REFERENCES

Berko, R. M., Rosenfeld, L. Bl, & Samovar, L. A. (1997). *Connecting: A culture-sensitive approach to interpersonal communication competency* (2nd ed.). Fort Worth, TX: Harcourt Brace College Publishers.

Bowers, J. (1997). Sequential patterns and the music teaching effectiveness of elementary education majors. *Journal of Research in Music Education, 45*, (3), 428-443.

Duke, R. A. (1999/2000). Measures of instructional effectiveness in music research. Council of Research in Music Education, 143, 1 - 49.

Dunn, D. E. (1997). Effect of rehearsal hierarchy and reinforcement on attention, achievement, and attitude of selected choirs. *Journal of Research in Music Education, 45,* 547-567.

Goolsby, T. W. (1997). Verbal instruction in instrumental rehearsals: A comparison of three career levels and preservice teachers. *Journal of Research in Music Education, 45,* 21-40.

Hamann, D. L., Baker, D. S., McAllister, P. A., & Bauer, W. I. (2000). Factors affecting university music students' perceptions of lesson quality and teaching effectiveness. *Journal of Research in Music Education, 48,* (2), 102-113.

Hendel, C. (1995). Behavioral characteristics and instructional patterns of selected music teachers. *Journal of Research in Music Education, 3,* (3), 182-203.

Lindsay, S. A. (2009). *Persuasion, proposals, and public speaking* (2nd ed.). Orlando, FL: Say Press.

References

Madsen, C. K. (1990). Teacher intensity in relationship to music education. *Council for Research in Music Education, 104,* 38 - 46.

Madsen, C. K., & Duke, R. A., (1993). Selection and development of prospective music teachers. *Journal of Music Teacher Education, 3 (1)*, 5-11.

Price, H. E. (1992) Sequential patterns of music instruction and learning to use them. *Journal of Research in Music Education, 40,* (1), 14-29.

Siebenaler, D. J. (1997). Analysis of teacher-student interactions in the piano lessons of adults and children. *Journal of Research in Music Education, 45,* 6-20.

Sims, W. L. (1986). The effect of high versus low teacher affect and passive versus active student activity during music listening on preschool children's attention, piece preference, time spent listening, and piece recognition. *Journal of Research in Music Education, 34,* (3), 173 - 191.

Speer, D. R. (1994). An analysis of sequential patterns of instruction in piano lessons. *Journal of Research in Music Education, 42,* (1), 14-26.

Yarbrough, C., & Price, H. E. (1981). Prediction of performer attentiveness based on rehearsal activity and teacher behavior. *Journal of Research in Music Education, 29,* (3), 209-217.

CONCEPT INDEX

Alberti Bass

    Alberti Calisthenics (22), p. 94

Arm/hand Independence

    Ear-Nose Name Game (25), p. 105

    Brain/Arm Teaser (26), p. 109

Arm/Wrist/Hand Movement

    Rockin' & Rollin' Frisbees (23), p. 116

    Hand-Crossing Pieces (27), p. 125

    Kneading Bread (28), p. 128

    Ear-nose Name Game (54), p. 185

    Brain/Arm Teaser (26), p.109

Baroque Imitation

    Baroque Imitation (31), p. 127

    Recreate this Photo (32), p. 131

Blues Scale (See also scales/arpeggios/technique)

    Blues Scale Hopscotch (10), p. 41

Chord Progressions

    Chord Progressions Scrabble (17), p. 71

Composition

    I Write the Songs (14), p. 59

Ensembles

> The Apprentice (27), p. 114

Harmonization

> Musical Pursuit (6), p. 26
>
> Chord Progressions Scrabble (17), p. 71
>
> Alberti Calisthenics (51), p. 179

Improvisation

> Musical Pursuit (6), p. 26
>
> Volleyball (7), p. 29
>
> The Gambler (15), p. 63
>
> The Shortest Distance Line (23), p. 98

Increasing Difficulty/Perfecting Musical Pieces

> Build a House (35), p. 143
>
> The Apprentice (27), p. 114
>
> Piano Arcade (4), p. 19
>
> Cross-Training (13), p. 54

Keys/Key Signatures

> Four Corners (9), p. 37
>
> Key Signature War (18), p. 75
>
> Triad Bingo (21), p. 89

Melodic Dictation

> Piano Telephone (12), p. 50

Musical Character

> Charade (Sort of) (16), p. 67
>
> Guests at a party (36), p. 150

Animated Feature (28), p. 117

Electric Statues (30), p. 124

Musical Styles and Forms

Recreate this Photo (32), p. 131

Classical Voices (33), p. 135

The Brown Suit (34), p. 139

Review

Horse (2), p. 12

Musical Pursuit (6), p. 26

The Natural (20), p. 85

Rote learning

I Write the Songs (14), p. 59

Scales/Arpeggios/Technique

Hurdles (5,) p. 23

Musical Pursuit (6), p. 26

Scale Fingering Dominoes (11), p. 46

Pentachord/Scale Game (19), p. 78

Grapevine Run (24), p. 101

Sight-reading

Prince of Paris (3), p. 15

Musical Pursuit (6), p. 26

Brain/Arm Teaser (26), p. 109

Tension/Relaxation

Stress Ball Pass (8), p. 33

Theme and Variations

    The Brown Suit (34), p. 139

Transposition

    Mother May I, p. 8

    Musical Pursuit (6), p. 26

Triads/Chords

    Triad Bingo (21), p. 89

www.ingramcontent.com/pod-product-compliance
Lightning Source LLC
Chambersburg PA
CBHW080736230426
43665CB00020B/2757